OXFORD
UNIVERSITY PRESS

Matrix
Computing for 11–14

Alison Page
Diane Levine
Steve Bunce
Areti Bizior

1

Matrix computing skills for the digital world

OXFORD

Great Clarendon Street, Oxford, OX2 6DP, United Kingdom

Oxford University Press is a department of the University of Oxford. It furthers the University's objective of excellence in research, scholarship, and education by publishing worldwide. Oxford is a registered trade mark of Oxford University Press in the UK and in certain other countries

British Library Cataloguing in Publication Data
Data available

ISBN 9780198395546

3 5 7 9 10 8 6 4

Paper used in the production of this book is a natural, recyclable product made from wood grown in sustainable forests. The manufacturing process conforms to the environmental regulations of the country of origin.

Printed in India by Manipal Technologies Limited

Acknowledgements

Thanks to:
Howard Lincoln, Educational Consultant and author, for chapters reviewed.
Dr Dov Stekel, Associate Professor of Integrative Systems Biology, Faculty of Science, University of Nottingham, for contributing ideas.
Chris Eccles, MSc, for technical fact checking.

Cover illustration: Koivo at Good Illustration

The publishers would like to thank the following for permissions to use their photographs:
p6-7: chairboy/iStockPhoto; p7: CHEN WS/Shutterstock.com; p12: monkeybusinessimages/iStockPhoto; p13: Pictorial Press Ltd/Alamy Stock Photo; p26: neftali/Shutterstock.com; p26b: famouspeople/Alamy Stock Photo; p35t: OUP/Shutterstock; p35: Andrew Brookes, National Physical Laboratory/Science Photo Library; p51: Jaroslav Moravcik/Shutterstock.com; p61: OUP/TongRo Image Stock; p62m: courtneyk/iStockPhoto; p62t: scyther5/iStockPhoto; p63: Pictorial Press Ltd/Alamy Stock Photo; p65: Photowitch/Dreamstime.com; p91t: Robert Kneschke/Fotolia; p90t: python.org; p91b: Pictorial Press Ltd/Alamy Stock Photo; p118-119: OUP/Photodisc; p118-119: kyoshino/iStockPhoto; p119b: anyaberkut/iStockPhoto; p119t: The IBM Main Frame 650 Computer(b/w photo)/Underwood Archives/UIG/Bridgeman Images; p120: pengpeng/iStockPhoto; p146t: Rick Friedman/Getty Images; p147: Flickr/Knight Foundation; p155: Rose Carson/Shutterstock.com; p162: bubaone/iStockPhoto.

All other photos by Shutterstock

Thanks to Wirify for allowing permission to reference their product.

Contents

Introduction

What this book is about

As a student, you need to understand how computers work. Most jobs in the future will need computer skills. Do you want to work in manufacturing, agriculture, fashion or perhaps education? What about computing? You might be one step away from creating the Internet's next big thing. Whatever you aim to do with your future, computers are everywhere and you will need to use them in some way.

This book will help you to develop your computer skills, so you can take your place in the world of work. It will help you learn to identify problems and solve them.

Even if you just want to use computers for fun, knowing how they work will help you to use them more creatively.

This book is divided into six chapters.

1   **Computational thinking:** Understanding a problem and thinking of the possible solutions is called computational thinking. Computational thinking teaches you a new way to think about the world by breaking problems down into smaller parts. Engineers, scientists, archaeologists, doctors and musicians all use computational thinking to solve problems.

2   App Inventor: If you have ever used your phone to play a game, send a message or listen to music, you have used application software (an app). An app is a set of instructions that make the computer inside your phone carry out a task. You will discover how to write your own apps for mobile phones using a programming language that works over the Internet.

3   Data and the CPU: What do the International Space Station and an electric toaster have in common? They both use the same basic computer technology. Today, computers are everywhere. Have you ever wondered how a computer works? You will find out how computers communicate and process information.

4   **Introducing Python:** You will learn to write in one of the programming languages that the professionals use. Python is a popular programming language that uses text-based commands to do many different tasks. You can use Python for just about anything from creating games to analysing research problems. Scientists and engineers at NASA use Python, and so do animators at Disney.

5 **Information technology:** You have probably used hardware and software in your everyday life. However, you may not know all the things hardware and software can do. You will learn how computer hardware and software work together. You will also learn how to protect yourself online and use the Internet responsibly.

6 **Creative communication:** Technology can help you get your ideas across to other people creatively. You will build a website to share information about your favourite subjects. Make your website eye-catching so that people will visit.

Learning by doing

In each chapter, you will learn by doing. The activities are designed to develop and stretch your ability. This is not a book to read while sitting and doing nothing. You will be challenged to write, make, create, discuss and invent.

Each chapter begins with an introduction to the theme. Six lessons follow. As you work through the lessons, you will learn new skills and develop your understanding. There are test questions and review activities at the end of each chapter. Answer the questions and complete the activities to show everything you have learned.

What you will find in each lesson

Each lesson takes four pages of the book. In each lesson you will find these sections.

Learn about... You will learn new facts and ideas about each subject.

How to... You will learn how to do new things and develop new skills.

Now you do it... There will be a chance to complete an activity, using your new skills.

If you have time... There are extension activities for students who work quickly and need extra challenges.

Test yourself... There are questions for you to answer to check your understanding of the topic.

Key words New words used in each lesson are explained.

1 Computational Thinking

Design a spam filter

Overview

Computers cannot think for themselves. In order to use computers to solve problems we have to think through the problem first. Making sure you understand a problem and thinking up possible solutions is called computational thinking.

In this chapter you will learn some basic principles of computational thinking and use them to design a simple spam filter.

Learning outcomes

By the end of this chapter you will know how to:

- describe computational thinking
- use decomposition to break a problem down into smaller parts
- describe an algorithm
- use pattern recognition
- use a flow chart to describe your problem-solving
- describe selection
- use `if... then... else` to navigate through a problem
- describe iteration
- use loops to navigate through a problem
- evaluate other people's work
- give helpful feedback.

Sent Mail

Spam (372)

Trash

Command Sequencing

Algorithm Elegant Implement

Data Efficient Computational
Fit for purpose Sequence thinking

Flow chart Criteria Process

Loop Selection

Spam filter Iteration Variable

Pattern recognition Spam

Decomposition

Learning outcomes

When you have completed this lesson you will be able to:

↗ describe computational thinking

↗ use decomposition to break a problem down into smaller parts.

⌘ Learn about...

Computational thinking is a **process** for solving problems. Using computational thinking, you can understand a problem and break it down into smaller parts. You can work out what is important and find a solution.

Your computational thinking toolbox has a set of useful tools for you to use.

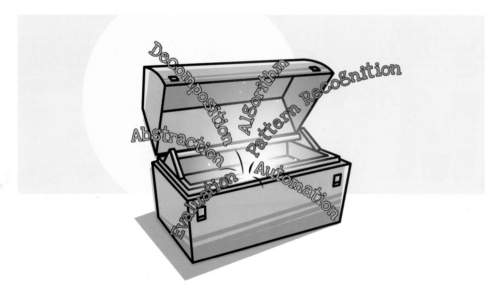

Decomposition and **algorithms** are two tools in your computational thinking toolbox.

Decomposition

Just as you would climb a mountain by taking one careful step at a time, you can decompose a problem by breaking it down into smaller parts. You can understand each part in more detail and solve it, one step at a time. If you do not decompose a problem, it can be harder to solve because you are trying to deal with too many parts at once.

Algorithm

An algorithm is a set of instructions or rules we can follow to carry out a task. We build algorithms by decomposing a problem so that we can carry out one task at a time. We carry out each task in a logical order.

⏻ How to...

You can use computational thinking to help break down a problem into smaller parts. This is called decomposition.

Imagine you are the manager of a chocolate factory and you want to make a new type of chocolate.

You would not just tell the workers to do anything they wanted! You would first decompose the problem into smaller parts.

↗   What type of chocolate would sell well?

↗   How would you make it?

↗   How would you get it to customers?

You can decompose the parts into even smaller parts until you have a list of simple tasks. You can then make a set of instructions to carry out each task.

What type of chocolate would sell well?

↗   Find out what type of chocolate customers would like to buy.

↗   How much would they be willing to pay for it?

How would we make it?

↗   Work out what ingredients and machines you would need to make the chocolate.

↗   Work with designers to create a wrapper.

↗   Test the chocolate.

↗   Set up a process in the factory for making the chocolate.

↗   Test the process.

How would we get it to customers?

↗   Get some shops to agree to stock the chocolate.

↗   Work out whether the chocolate should get to the shops by rail, air or road.

↗   Make the chocolate.

↗   Transport the chocolate to the shops.

The sets of instructions here are algorithms. This is an algorithm for the task: Find out what type of chocolate customers would like to buy.

1   Invent some chocolate ideas.

2   Make a poster of each chocolate.

3   Find a group of people to look at the ideas.

4   Show them the chocolate ideas.

5   Give them a survey to say which idea they like best.

You can use decomposition in computer programming in exactly the same way. You can break your problem down into small chunks and carry out one task at a time. This can save time. If there is a mistake in a program with many lines of computer code, you can check each section of code separately.

Now you do it...

In this chapter you are going to design a simple **spam filter**. Email **spam** involves sending messages to many people who have not asked for the emails to be sent. We call this unsolicited email. Spam emails often contain links that look as if they might be from well-known and trusted websites, such as a bank's website. A spam filter is a computer program that spots unsolicited email. A spam filter can stop unsolicited email from getting into your inbox. Your spam filter will detect spam relating to online banking, and will also spot emails from a bank that ask for personal details. Any email you receive that asks for personal banking details is likely to be untrustworthy.

From: jstyles@cooltunes.com

Heading: Stranded in Florida

How are you doing? We have not been introduced, but I need your help and have no one else to turn to. I have had to send this in a rush because I am in desperate trouble.

My family and I visited Florida for a short vacation recently and we were mugged outside our hotel. The thieves stole all our cash, cell phones and credit cards. Now we can't go home because we can't pay our hotel bill. We are stranded!

Would you please urgently send a cheque for any amount you can spare (even $100 would help) to a temporary post office box that we have set up? The address is below:

PO Box 2014
Maple Bay
Florida, USA 02956
I really need your help. Thank you.

Your friend,

Mrs Smith

 HONEST BANK

HONEST BANK™ jstyles@honestbank.cooltunes.com

6:30 AM (10 hours ago)

Dear Valued Customer

We understand that you have withdrawn $5,000 from your checking account while in another country.

If this information is incorrect, someone you do not know may be using your account.

Please visit our website and give us your account details so that we can be sure all the information we have for you is correct.

Click here to update your details. www.cqhy457.com

Thank you for banking with us.

Yours sincerely

Honest Bank

What are the differences between an honest email and a fake one?

Work with a partner to answer these questions. Use the email examples from Honest Bank and Mrs Smith to help you.

- ↗ Who is the email from? Does the name on the email match the email address?
- ↗ Is the content of the email addressed to the email owner?
- ↗ Does the email ask for personal details?
- ↗ Does the email ask for money?
- ↗ What are the key words that your spam filter will detect?

When you answer these questions, you decompose the problem of understanding the differences between an honest email and a fake one. You can use the information to help you in future work.

If you have time...

Work with a partner. Each of you should make a list of four items. Three items on your list should have things in common and one item should be the odd one out. For example, you could choose a baseball, a tennis ball, a balloon and a basketball.

Which is the odd one out? The balloon is the odd one out because you cannot play a sport with a balloon.

The balloon does have something in common with the other items. All of the items can be spherical.

Can your partner identify the odd one out on your list? Why is it the odd one out? Can you think of something all four things have in common?

Test yourself...

1 What is an algorithm?
2 Decompose the problem of getting dressed in the morning.
3 What should you do if you receive a spam email?
4 Give an example of how computational thinking is relevant to everyday life.

Key words

Algorithm: An algorithm is a set of instructions or rules that we can follow to carry out a task.

Computational thinking: Computational thinking is a way of thinking through problems and finding good solutions for them. We can apply the principles of computational thinking to computer programs and to solving problems in our everyday lives.

Decomposition: Decomposition is breaking a problem down into smaller parts.

Process: A process is a set of steps we can take to solve a problem or reach a goal. A process can include a set of algorithms to solve a problem.

Spam: Email spam involves sending messages to many people who have not asked for the emails to be sent.

Spam filter: A spam filter is a computer program that spots unsolicited email. A spam filter can stop unsolicited email from getting into your inbox.

Learning outcomes

When you have completed this lesson you will be able to:

↗ use pattern recognition.

⌘ Learn about...

Look at these people.

They are all different. Look closer. Do you see there are things that are similar between them? For example, they all have:

↗ eyes
↗ a nose
↗ a mouth
↗ teeth.

These are all features on a face that people have in common. In computational thinking we call these common features a pattern.

Being able to identify and describe a pattern is an important part of computational thinking. Identifying and describing patterns is also important in our everyday lives.

Why is it important to identify patterns?

He was a Hungarian doctor who worked in a hospital where babies were being born. At that time, many women having babies in hospitals died of an illness called puerperal fever. Semmelweiss worked in the First Clinic at the hospital. This is where medical students were trained to deliver babies. In another clinic at the hospital, the Second Clinic, midwives were trained to deliver babies. Semmelweiss saw that more women died in the First Clinic than in the Second Clinic.

This is Ignaz Semmelweiss (1818–1865)

Semmelweiss decided to try to find out why so many women were dying in the First Clinic. He wrote down all the similarities and differences between the two clinics. For example, he studied the number of patients and the climate in both clinics. He could not find any patterns that would explain the high death rate in the First Clinic.

Then one of his doctor friends died after cutting his finger during an autopsy, which is an examination of a dead body. Semmelweiss knew that almost all of the medical students did autopsies. Student midwives did not. In those days doctors did not wear gloves or wash their hands. Semmelweiss realised that the medical students were taking something dangerous from the dead bodies to the women patients in the First Clinic. He told all of his colleagues to start washing their hands after autopsies. The death rate in the First Clinic dropped by 90 per cent. The fall in the death rate happened because Semmelweiss had found the pattern and then the right solution.

Patterns and computational thinking

Pattern recognition is finding the similarities and differences between things. You can use pattern recognition to help write algorithms. If you do not look for patterns when you decompose your problems, you might take longer to find the right solution or you might not find the right solution at all.

We often ask computers to recognise patterns for us.

 **How to...**

You are designing a spam filter in this chapter. You can do this by finding a set of features that helps you tell the difference between spam and non-spam email. You can write an algorithm that tells the computer to look for these differences in your emails.

What kinds of words or phrases do you think you would find in spam emails? Here are some examples.

bargain	million	dear friend	opportunity
money	billion	fees	cost
fast	debt	credit card	urgent
please read	please help	$ or other currency symbol	funds
bank	guarantee	rates	income

Many spam emails use these words and phrases. Computer algorithms can spot these words across many possible spam emails. The algorithm is finding a word pattern. If an email has many of these types of words, it is possible that it is a spam email.

 **Now you do it...**

Look at your decomposed spam filter problem.

↗ Can you identify any patterns that might be useful?

↗ What parts of the email could you think of as patterns?

Remember that there may be patterns in an individual spam email. For example, you might notice the repeated use of a fake business name or email account. There may also be patterns between several spam emails. For example, spam emails may ask for personal banking details.

 **If you have time...**

Work with a partner. Compare making a cup of tea with making a cup of instant coffee. Which tasks are similar? Which tasks are different? Where could you use the same instructions in both processes?

Test yourself...

1 What is pattern recognition?

2 Look at the image of some robots on the next page. Write any patterns you see.

In Lesson 1.1 you decomposed the problem of designing and selling a new type of chocolate. Now imagine you are also going to design and sell a new type of cake.

3   Decompose the cake problem.

4   Write the patterns you can see between the chocolate design process and the cake design process.

Key words

Pattern recognition: Pattern recognition is finding things that decomposed problems have in common.

Learning outcomes

When you have completed this lesson you will be able to:

↗ describe an algorithm

↗ use a flow chart to describe your problem-solving.

⌘ Learn about...

You know that an algorithm is a set of instructions or rules you can follow to carry out a task. You can use algorithmic thinking to work through and solve problems.

A computer cannot think for itself. We must do the thinking to design algorithms so that the computer has instructions to follow. When we give the computer a correct algorithm, it will work on the problems we want it to solve.

Computer programs that are given incorrect or inefficient algorithms will not work well. An inefficient algorithm means the computer has to work harder to solve the problem. Computer programs work well when they are given carefully planned algorithms. In a well-designed algorithm, each instruction is clear. The order for carrying out instructions is also clear.

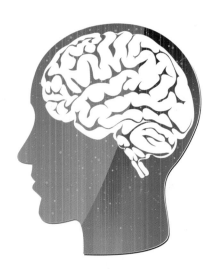

What is a flow chart?

Writing algorithms as long lists is not a good way of communicating a set of instructions. Why do you think that is?

A list is not a good way of giving a set of instructions because it does not show the relationships between the steps needed to carry out a task. You can use a **flow chart** instead. A flow chart is a diagram that explains a process. Each step in the process is shown in a box. Different types of box mean different actions.

How to...

We use symbols in flow charts to show what action to take.

 This shape shows the beginning and end of a **sequence**. A sequence is the order in which one task follows another.

 This shape shows a **command**. A command is a specific instruction.

 This shape shows a 'yes' or 'no' decision.

 This shape shows where **data** are being received or sent from a computer program. Data are facts and figures.

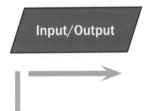 These arrows show the way we move through the sequence from symbol to symbol. The arrows show the direction of flow.

A **variable** is anything that can be stored by the computer, and changed, controlled or measured. We use variables in flow charts to show what is being changed, controlled or measured in our algorithm.

Making a flow chart

This is a flow chart for a simple program that shows whether a named user likes reading. The user is the person who is using the program.

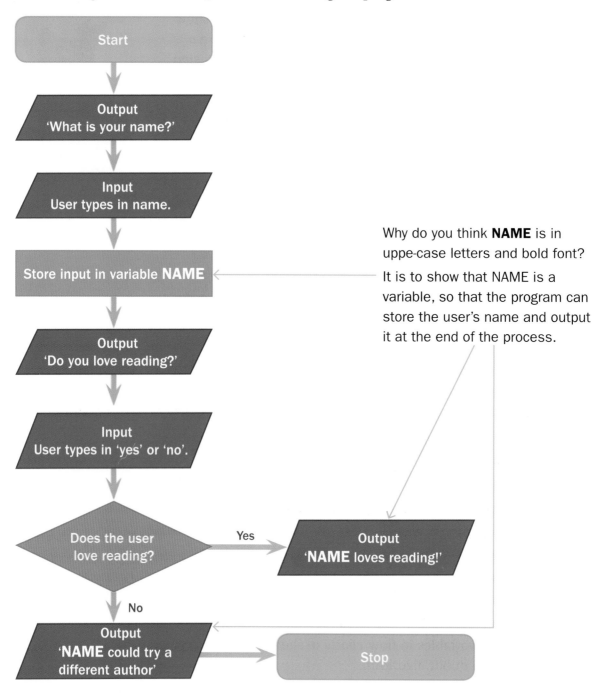

Why do you think **NAME** is in uppe-case letters and bold font?

It is to show that NAME is a variable, so that the program can store the user's name and output it at the end of the process.

⊕ Now you do it...

Make a flow chart to describe the program for your spam filter. Remember that your spam filter is going to try to detect spam relating to online banking.

↗ Look at your decomposition of the spam filter problem.
↗ Work with a partner to decide on symbols to represent each step in your flow chart.

For example, when your program scans an incoming email to see whether it contains the word 'MONEY', would that be a process or a decision, or both? First the program would need to carry out a process for scanning the incoming email. You could show the process as:

Then the program would need to make a decision about whether or not the email contained the word 'MONEY'. You could show the decision as:

If you have time...

Can you think of any disadvantages of using flow charts to show your computational thinking?

Test yourself...

1 Why are flow charts useful in computational thinking?
2 Draw and label the four main shapes we use to make flow charts.
3 Decompose the task of brushing your teeth.
4 Make a flow chart to describe the process of brushing your teeth.

F|A|C|T

Flow charts are not just used in computing. Project managers, engineers, designers and surgeons all use flow charts in their work.

Key words

Command: A command is an instruction that tells the computer to do something.

Data: Data are facts and figures.

Flow chart: A flow chart is a diagram that explains a process. Each step in the process is shown in a box. Different types of box mean different actions.

Sequence: A sequence is the order in which one task follows another.

Variable: A variable is anything that can be changed, controlled or measured.

Selection and `if... then... else` **statements**

Learning outcomes

When you have completed this lesson you will be able to:

↗ describe selection

↗ use `if... then... else` to navigate through a problem.

⌘ Learn about...

You already know that an algorithm is a set of instructions or rules that you can use to solve a problem or carry out a task. We write computer programs to **implement** algorithms. To implement an algorithm means to put it into action.

You also know that we can use flow charts to represent the sequence of instructions in an algorithm. **Sequencing** is one tool that you can use to design algorithms. Another tool is **selection**.

↗ Selection can be a decision. Decision

↗ Selection can be a question.

Selection happens when you reach a step in the algorithm that has two or more possibilities. The program then needs to ask a question. Depending on the answer to the question, the program chooses a particular direction of flow. The program will ignore any other possibility. This selects the path through the flow chart.

Selection

You can use your flow charts to show choices and decisions as questions. The flow chart can show what would happen if the answer to the question is 'yes' or 'no'.

 How to...

Using the example from Lesson 1.3, the algorithm's message depends on whether you enjoy reading. This is how we might show selection in plain English.

1 Ask whether the user loves reading.
2 `if` the user loves reading, `then` say, 'NAME loves reading!'
3 Or `else` say, 'NAME could try a different author.'

We can show these statements in a flow chart using selection.

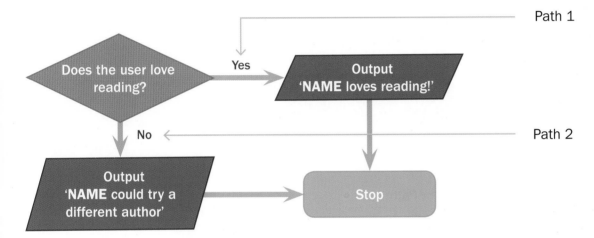

The green shape is the question. `if` the answer is 'yes', `then` the output is 'NAME loves reading!'

`if` the answer is 'no', `then` the output is 'NAME could try a different author.'

Many computer programs use the words `if`, `then` and `else` to make a selection.

Sometimes you will want to show more than two paths in answer to a question.

In our example, we ask whether the user loves reading. Some users will love reading. Some users will only like reading. Some users will not love or like reading at all.

Using our example:

Ask whether the user loves reading.

if the user loves reading, then say 'NAME loves reading!'

Or else if the user likes reading, then say 'NAME does not feel strongly about reading.'

Or else say 'NAME could try a different author.'

This is path 1 on the flow chart.

This is path 2 on the flow chart.

This is path 3 on the flow chart.

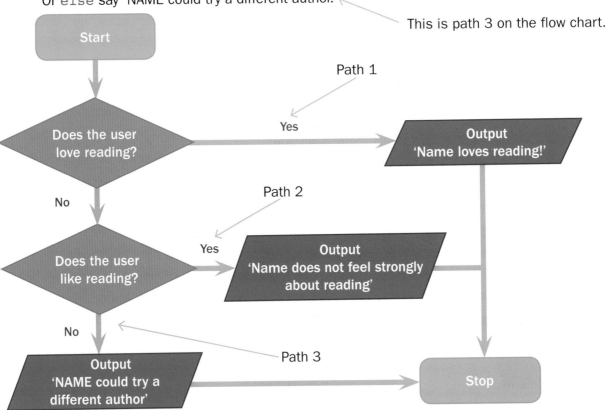

⊕ Now you do it...

Work with your partner. Apply what you know about selection to the flow chart showing your design of a spam filter.

When you reach your decision points, think of the possible answers to the question. Show the different paths your design could take.

🌐 If you have time...

Can you think of any other examples of computer programs where selection would be useful?

📄 Test yourself...

1 Finish this sentence: Selection happens when…

2 What does implement mean?

3   Work with a partner. Imagine you are programming a game. Your avatar is walking along a woodland path. The avatar sees three paths ahead. Decompose the problem. Are there obstacles on any of the paths? Is there treasure on any of the paths?

4   Create a simple flow chart that shows what your avatar sees when looking down each one of the paths.

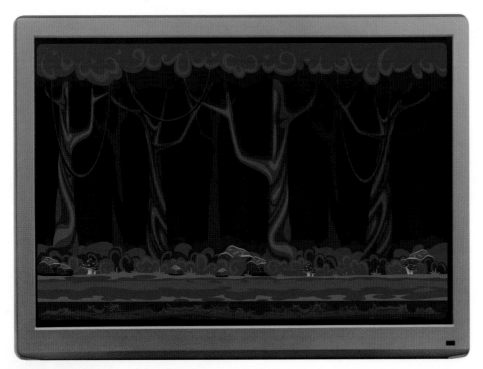

Key words

Implement: Implement means to put algorithms into action.

Selection: Selection happens when you reach a step in the algorithm where the program has two or more possibilities of what to do next.

Sequencing: Sequencing is the order in which steps or tasks are carried out.

Learning outcomes

When you have completed this lesson you will be able to:

↗ describe iteration

↗ use loops in a program.

⌘ Learn about...

You already know about two tools that we can use to design algorithms. These are sequencing and selection. Computer scientists call these tools programming constructs. Constructs are the tools that you can use to build algorithms.

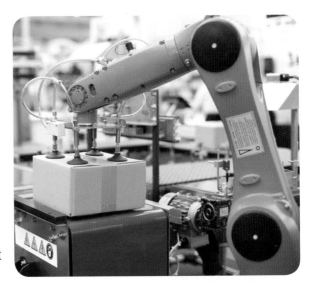

In this lesson you will learn about another important tool, called **iteration**.

Sometimes an algorithm has to repeat a step. For example, imagine you are programming a robot to work in a factory. The robot picks up an item and puts it down somewhere else. The robot then moves back to the first position and picks up the next item, and so on. The robot needs to repeat the motion steps many times.

We call this iteration.

Loops

Using iteration, we do not need to write out the same instruction many times. We can simply say that we will repeat (or iterate) particular steps until we tell the algorithm to stop.

Most programmers use the word **loop** when they talk about iteration. When a program iterates, it loops back to a previous step.

Iteration is an important element of computational thinking. You can apply it to almost any activity in your everyday life. For example, if you want to become good at playing a musical instrument you need to practise. For each piece of music you learn to play, you need to repeat sections. You improve each time you repeat correctly.

 **How to...**

Imagine your avatar from Lesson 1.4 sees treasure down each woodland path and wants to collect it. How might you represent this in a flow chart?

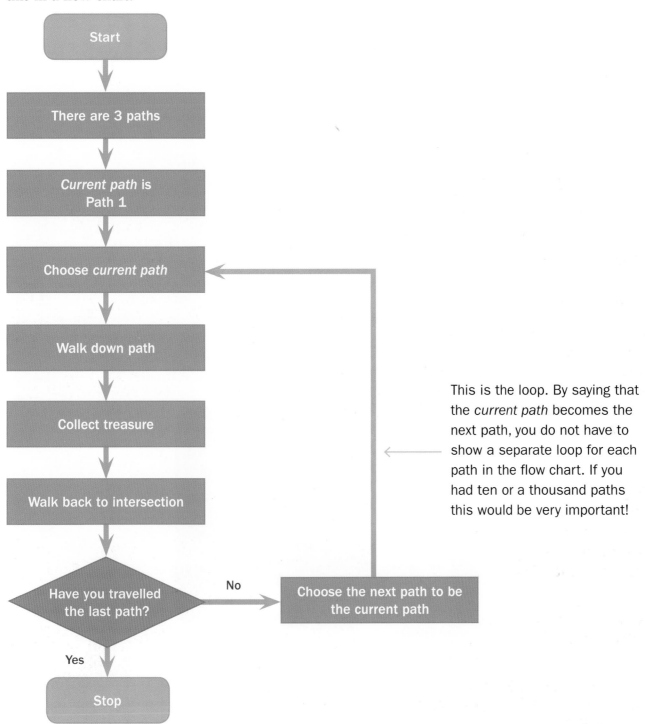

The flow chart starts by stating that there are three paths. The flow chart defines the current path as Path 1. The avatar is instructed to walk down the current path. The avatar collects the treasure. The avatar walks back to the starting point. The loop means that the next path is now the current path. After Path 1 comes Path 2, then Path 3.

⊕ Now you do it...

Work with your partner. Apply what you know about loops to the flow chart that describes your spam filter program. You may want to change your flow chart in some way. Ask yourself these questions.

↗ Where are there repeated actions in your flow chart? For example, do you want your spam filter to repeat a sequence of steps for a second email, or more?

↗ Can you show these in a more efficient and elegant way by using loops?

↗ Do you need to say how many loops there will be?

🌐 If you have time...

How would you change the flow chart if you had ten paths? How would you change it if you had one million paths?

📄 Test yourself...

1 Complete the words naming the three algorithm constructs we use in computational thinking:

S _____   S _____   I _____

2 Why is iteration important in programming?

FA**C**T

Alan Turing (1912–1954)

Alan Turing was a famous British mathematician and early computer scientist. In 1936 he invented the Turing machine, which is an idea-based model of how a computer could work. The Turing machine would not work without the idea of iteration.

3   Think of an example of a computer program that needs to use loops.

4   Using your own words, describe what is happening in this flow chart.

CLUE: This is a factory robot.

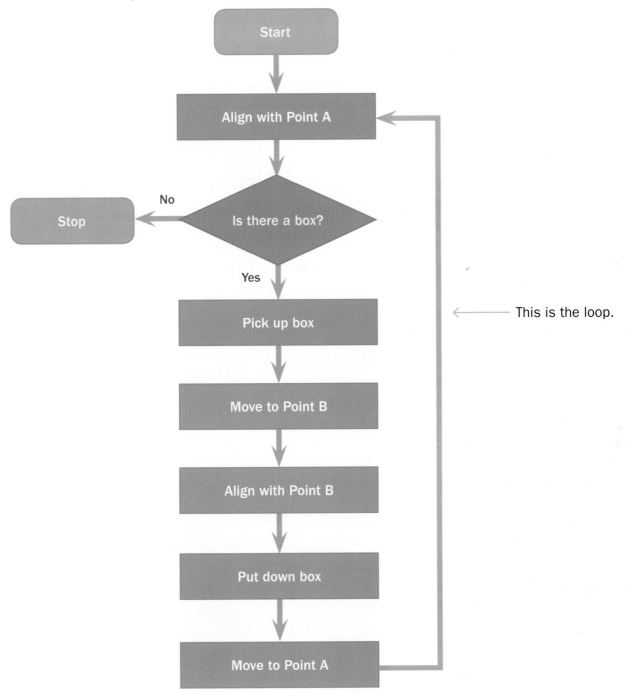

Key words

Iteration: Iteration means repeating a step or task in an algorithm or computer program.

Loop: To loop means to go back to a previous step. Looping happens in iteration.

Evaluation

Learning outcomes

When you have completed this lesson you will be able to:

↗ evaluate other people's work

↗ give helpful feedback.

⌘ Learn about...

Once you have decomposed a problem and developed a possible solution, it is time to evaluate what you have done. You need to be sure that the solution is **fit for purpose**. This means that the solution is able to completely solve the problem.

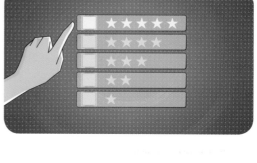

Sometimes, when you have been working on an idea, it is difficult to look at your work critically. You have worked so hard that it is not easy to see where the faults are. There are two simple ways to deal with this.

1   You can evaluate your design against set **criteria**. The criteria are the things to judge the program against. You can use criteria to tell you whether a program works well or not.

2   You can pass your design to someone else so that person can test it and give you helpful feedback.

⏻ How to...

A good algorithm should have characteristics that fit together like a jigsaw puzzle.

As you write an algorithm, you need to ask whether the problem has been properly decomposed. Decomposed means being broken down into parts. **Efficient** means doing the best work for the least effort. **Elegant** means that the algorithm is very clear for someone else to understand. Correct means that there are no mistakes in the algorithm.

If an algorithm has all of these pieces it can solve the whole problem quickly, using as little work as possible. If you have agreed design criteria at the start of a project, it is easier to evaluate an algorithm. If you do not have agreed design criteria, these puzzle pieces are a good place to start.

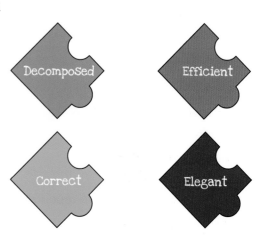

Here is an example of someone starting to make a cup of tea. Can you see where the process might be improved?

Using this feedback, the algorithm could look like this:

Take a cup out of the cupboard.

Put in a teabag.

Turn on the kettle.

The algorithm is not correct. There are some steps missing. The process could be improved by thinking through the decomposed problem more carefully.

The algorithm is not elegant. For example, it is not clear where the cupboard is.

The algorithm is not properly decomposed, so it is not efficient. It could be improved by breaking the steps down further. For example, break the algorithm down further with these steps: getting a cup, getting water, choosing what kind of tea. Each of these steps would also have steps within it.

Getting a cup
- Take a cup out of the cupboard in the kitchen.
- Put the cup on the table.

Getting water
- Pick up the kettle.
- Take the kettle to the sink.
- Turn on the tap.
- Pour water into the kettle.
- Turn off the tap.
- Return the kettle to the plug.
- Heat the water in the kettle.

Choosing tea
- Walk to the cupboard that has tea in it.
- Open the cupboard.
- Look at the kinds of tea in the cupboard.
- Pick up the mint herbal teabags.
- Close the cupboard.
- Walk to the cup.
- Put a mint herbal teabag in the cup.

1 Pick up the kettle

2 Take the kettle to the sink

3 Turn on the tap

Giving others feedback

There are three important things to remember when you are evaluating other people's work and giving them feedback.

Keep it about the work
Don't say: Your work is dull.
Do say: You could make your algorithm shorter by adding a loop here.

Show where things are working well
Point out things that have been done well.

Giving helpful feedback

Be specific
Don't say: You've missed some steps.
Do say: You need to add steps here and here.

⊕ Now you do it...

By now, you should have a spam filter design that is ready to share.

1 Work in a group. Develop evaluation criteria for your spam filters. Is your design efficient, correct, decomposed and elegant?

2 Now use your criteria to evaluate the design of another group. Show where the design is strong. Show the areas that need improvement.

3 Give your feedback to the other group.

If you have time...

Improve your algorithm based on the feedback you have been given.

Test yourself...

1 What criteria can we use to judge whether an algorithm is fit for purpose?
2 What are the characteristics of good feedback?
3 Summarise the main strengths and weaknesses of the spam filter you have designed.
4 How could you address the weaknesses?

Key words

Criteria: The criteria are the things to judge a program against.

Efficient: Efficient means doing the best work for the least effort.

Elegant: Elegant means to be very clear for someone else to understand.

Fit for purpose: Fit for purpose means that a program does the job it is supposed to do.

Review what you have learned about computational thinking

Overview

In this chapter you learned some basic principles of computational thinking. You used computational thinking principles to design a simple spam filter. You have learned how to:

- ↗ describe computational thinking
- ↗ use decomposition to break a problem down into smaller parts
- ↗ describe an algorithm
- ↗ use pattern recognition
- ↗ use a flow chart to describe your problem-solving

- ↗ describe selection
- ↗ use `if... then... else` to navigate through a problem
- ↗ describe iteration
- ↗ use loops to navigate through a problem
- ↗ evaluate other people's work
- ↗ give helpful feedback.

 Test questions

Answer these questions to check how well you have learned this topic.

1 What is computational thinking?

2 Why is computational thinking important to programming?

3 Give an example of how you can use computational thinking in everyday life.

4 What are the three constructs you can use to design algorithms?

5 Explain what these words and phrases mean using your own words.

   a pattern recognition   **c** selection

   b sequencing   **d** iteration

6 What is a loop?

7 Give an example of an algorithm where a loop would be useful.

8 **a** Think back to the algorithm evaluation jigsaw. Which four words can you use to help decide whether an algorithm is fit for purpose?

   b On a separate sheet of paper, draw the jigsaw and write one of the four words you have chosen on each piece.

9 Design a poster to tell other students about the dangers of spam. Include this information on your poster.

   a What is spam?

   b What is a spam filter?

   c How does a spam filter work?

   d What should you do if you receive a spam email?

10 Look at the poster another student has made. Evaluate the poster by telling the other student one thing that has been done well, and one thing that the student could do to improve the poster.

Assessment activities

Imagine you want to make a simple meal.

| Perhaps you want to make a sandwich. | Perhaps you want to make a salad. | Perhaps you want to make a boiled egg. |

Starter activity

✓ Choose one of these meals and decompose the task of making the meal.

Intermediate activity

✓ Draw a flow chart to show how you would make the meal.

Extension activity

✓ Look at the flow chart made by a partner.

✓ Evaluate your partner's flow chart. Give your partner helpful feedback on how to improve the flow chart.

App Inventor

Make a mobile app

Overview

Most phones and other mobile devices run apps. App is short for application software. An app is a set of instructions that control the computer. The instructions make the computer carry out a useful task. In this chapter you will make an app that displays an ID card on an Android phone.

Learning outcomes

By the end of this chapter you will know how to create a simple app. You will use the App Inventor programming language, which runs on Android phones. You will know how to:

- ↗ design an interface with buttons, labels and text boxes
- ↗ make an event-driven program that reacts to user commands
- ↗ display text and images as output from a computer program
- ↗ describe syntax errors and other error messages
- ↗ duplicate and delete code blocks
- ↗ upload and use multimedia content
- ↗ use logical tests and the `if` command to control the computer
- ↗ test and evaluate a program to see whether it meets user needs.

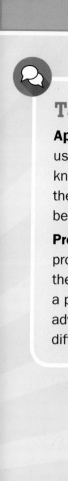

Talk about...

Apps: There are millions of apps available to use on mobile phones. What apps do you know? What are the most useful apps? Are there any apps you would like that haven't been invented yet?

Proof of identity (ID): You often have to prove your ID, for example when you go into the school building. What ways are there for a person to prove his or her ID? What are the advantages and disadvantages of the different methods?

Design an ID card

In this chapter you will make an on-screen ID card that shows your name and image. Work in pairs or small groups to make a draft design for an ID card. What extra information would you show as well as name and photo?

Employee ID
Electro Corporation Inc

8990
6402

Vanessa Chang
Customer Services Advisor

Images avail: 3

F= 98.00%   S= 96%
T= 18   N=209

App

Event-driven programming

Upload   **Input**   Syntax   Property

Text property   **Output**

Evaluate   Client

Trigger

Right-click

Syntax error   **Logical test**

Visual programming

Multimedia

Design the touch-screen interface

Learning outcomes

In this chapter you will make an app for a phone. Your app will display your ID on the screen of a mobile phone. In this lesson you will start to design the screen.

When you have completed this lesson you will be able to:

↗ design an interface with buttons and labels.

⌘ Learn about...

In this chapter you will write a program using App Inventor. You will:

↗ design the screen of the **app**

↗ write program code that goes with the app.

Interface

An interface is the part of a program that helps the human user. The interface lets you send a message to the computer. This is called **input**. The interface lets the computer send a message to you. This is called **output**.

A modern mobile phone has a computer inside it. The screen of the phone is used for input and output. The user touches the screen to control the computer. That is input. The computer shows words and images on the screen. That is output.

Interface design

You will make an interface that will have a button and a label. When you click the button, the label will show your name.

 How to...

To get started, log in to the App Inventor website. Your teacher will show you how. At the top is a menu bar.

↗ **Open the first menu, Projects, and select Start new project**

↗ **Give your first project a one-word name, such as IDCard**

The project will be linked to your personal login details. Nobody else will be able to see it.

Designer

Below the menu bar is the Designer screen. This is where you will design the interface for your app.

The Designer screen is split into four sections. Running from left to right, these are:

1 Palette   **3** Components

2 Viewer   **4** Properties

You will use all four sections to make the interface.

Palette

The Palette shows a list of different objects. You can use these objects to make an interface. You drag objects from the Palette onto the Viewer.

↗ **Drag a Button and a Label onto the Viewer**

Viewer

You see the interface design on the Viewer. There are now two objects on the interface: a Button and a Label.

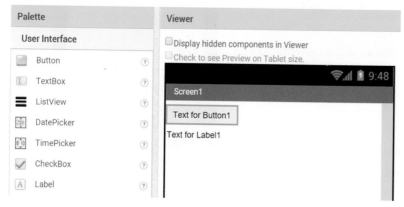

Components

The Components section lists the objects you have added to the interface.

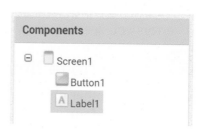

The objects are called Button1 and Label1. You can change the names to IDButton and NameLabel. These names will help you remember what the objects are for.

↗ **Select Button1**

↗ **Find the Rename button at the bottom of the Components list Click the Rename button**

↗ **Type the new name for the object** `IDButton`

↗ **Click OK**

↗ **Now change the name of Label1 to** `NameLabel`

Properties

The final section of the screen is called Properties. Every object has properties. A **property** is any feature of an object, such as its colour or size. You can change the properties of an object, such as the **text property**. That means the text that is written on an object.

- ↗ **Select** `IDButton`
- ↗ **Look down the Properties column until you find the Text property box**
- ↗ **Type** `Click for ID`
- ↗ **Change the text property of** `NameLabel` **to** `Name:`

Now, when you look at the Viewer the objects show the text property you gave them.

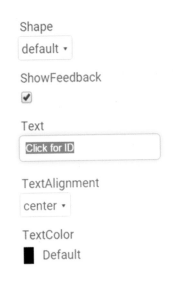

Run the app

You can run the app you made using one of two methods.

- ↗ Use the App Inventor Emulator on your computer. You will see an image like a mobile phone screen on your computer.
- ↗ Use the App Inventor Companion. You will need a mobile device with a wireless connection. You will see the app on the screen on the mobile device.

Your teacher will tell you which method to use. When you run the app you will see the interface you made.

The interface does not do anything yet. In Lesson 2.2 you will add code so that it works as an ID system.

⊕ Now you do it...

1 Start App Inventor. Create an interface with a button and a label. Give the objects suitable names. Set the text properties of the objects.

2 Run the app and check the interface you made. Correct any errors you see.

🌐 If you have time...

- ↗ There are other object properties, for example background colour and font size. Change some of these properties. See if you can improve the appearance of the interface.
- ↗ If you click Screen1 you can change the colour of the screen itself.

📄 Test yourself...

1   What is the difference between input and output?

2   Every object in App Inventor has properties. List three properties that an object might have.

3   The interface you made has two objects. Which object is used for input and which for output?

4   You changed the names of two objects. What makes a good name for an object?

FACT

App Inventor

App Inventor is a programming language that is available free on the Internet. App Inventor is provided by a university called the Massachusetts Institute of Technology (MIT). Anyone on the Internet is allowed to use App Inventor. You use App Inventor to make apps for mobile phones.

FACT

Naming objects

The name of an object must be one word with no spaces. The name of an object should explain what it is and what it does. The button on this app will show your ID. The button could be named IDButton.

Key words

App: App is short for application software. An app is a set of instructions that control the computer. Apps are created by programmers using a programming language.

Input: Input means signals and information sent from the user to the computer.

Output: Output means signals and information sent from the computer to the user.

Property: A property of an object is any of its features, such as its colour or size.

Text property: The text property of an object means the words written on it.

Learning outcomes

You have made an app interface with two objects on it. Now you will write program code. The code will make the app carry out actions in response to user input.

When you have completed this lesson you will be able to:

↗ make an **event-driven program** that reacts to user commands

↗ display text as output from a computer program.

⌘ Learn about...

In this lesson you will write program code. The code will tell the computer to show your name on the screen. You will make the code by fitting blocks together.

The code is carried out when the user clicks the button called IDButton. An event that makes the computer carry out an action is called a **trigger**. Clicking IDButton is a trigger.

⏻ How to...

Make sure your app is open in the web browser. Look at the top right of the screen. There are two buttons. These buttons let you swap between two different views.

↗ Designer: this screen is where you make the interface.

↗ Blocks: this screen is where you make the program code.

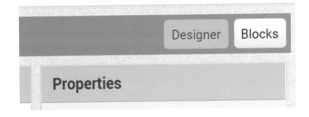

↗ **Select the Blocks button**

The Blocks screen has two sections: Blocks and Viewer. You choose blocks from the Blocks section and then drag blocks onto the Viewer section. You can build up the code by fitting blocks together.

`IDButton`

You can make code that is triggered when the user clicks `IDButton`.

In the Blocks section you will see a list of different types of block. At the bottom of the list find `IDButton`.

↗ **Click** `IDButton`

When you select `IDButton` you will see a range of blocks. These blocks are all linked to `IDButton`.

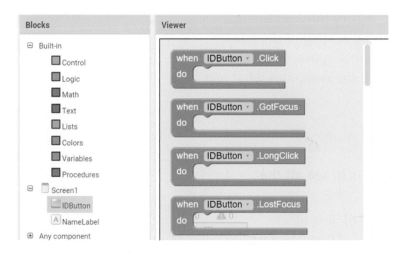

↗ **Select the top block called** `when  IDButton.Click`

↗ **Position this block on the Viewer**

Your screen now looks like this.

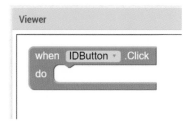

The block has a space that you can put blocks into. These blocks tell the computer what to do. When the user clicks `IDButton`, the computer will carry out these actions.

Set `NameLabel` **text**

When users click `IDButton` their name will appear in `NameLabel`. This means you need a block that will set the text property of `NameLabel`.

↗ **Look in the Blocks section**

↗ **Click** `NameLabel`

You will see a range of blocks on the screen. The blocks are all linked to NameLabel.

↗ **Scroll down through the list to find the block that lets you set the text property of** `NameLabel`

↗ **Drag this block onto the Viewer**

↗ **Put the** `NameLabel` **block inside** `when IDButton.Click`

It will fit exactly into the space in the other block. Fitting the blocks together is like completing a jigsaw.

These blocks mean 'When the user clicks IDButton, set the text property of NameLabel.' There is a warning symbol at the bottom left of the blocks screen. The warning symbol appears because your task is not finished yet. Now you must tell the computer what text to show in `NameLabel`.

Add new text

↗ **Look in the Blocks section**

↗ **Find the pink Text category. Click this to see all the Text blocks**

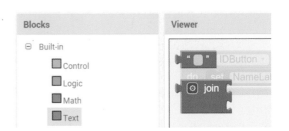

The block you need is at the top of the list of Text blocks. The block has an empty space where you can type any text.

↗ **Drag the empty Text block onto the Viewer**

↗ **Fit it into the** `NameLabel` **block**

↗ **Put your name in the empty space**

In this example we are using the name `Pharaoh Tutankhamun`. Use your own name or any name you like. The program blocks now look like this:

These blocks mean 'When the user clicks IDButton, set the text property of NameLabel to Pharaoh Tutankhamun.' The program is finished.

Run the app

Run the app you made to see what it looks like. Remember there are two ways to do this. You can use the App Inventor Emulator on your computer, or you can use the App Inventor Companion on a wireless device. Click `IDButton` and your name will be displayed on the screen.

 Now you do it...

1 Use the Blocks screen to create a simple program. The program will show your name when you click `IDButton`.

2 Run the app to check that it works and correct any errors.

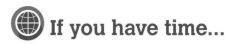 **If you have time...**

You can add extra blocks inside `when IDButton.Click`. When the user clicks `IDButton`, these extra commands will be carried out.

✎ Extend the program interface to include more labels. These can display extra facts such as date of birth or school name. Give these objects suitable names.

✎ Add extra code blocks inside `when IDButton.Click`. These extra blocks will change the text in the new labels that you added. When the user clicks `IDButton` he or she will see the new text in these labels.

```
when  IDButton ▾ .Click
do    set  NameLabel ▾ . Text ▾  to  " Pharaoh Tutankhamun "
      set  DateOfBirthLabel ▾ . Text ▾  to  " 1340 BC "
      set  JobLabel ▾ . Text ▾  to  " King of Egypt "
```

📝 **Test yourself...**

1 Why do you think App Inventor is sometimes called a **visual programming** language?

2 The code you made is triggered when an event happens. What event triggers the action?

3 Explain the purpose of the Designer screen and the Blocks screen in App Inventor. What is the difference between them?

4 When the trigger happens, what action is carried out by the computer?

Key words

Event-driven program: Computer software can be event driven. This means the actions of the software are triggered by events. Until the event happens the software won't do anything. App Inventor is an event-driven programming language.

Visual programming: Visual programming means that you make the program by fitting shapes together. App Inventor is a visual programming language.

Trigger: A trigger is an event that causes the computer to carry out an action.

Reset button

Learning outcomes

You have made a simple interface. You have added program code. In this lesson you will add an extra button to the interface, plus code to make it work. This is a Reset button. When the user presses the Reset button the text of `NameLabel` will blank out.

When you have completed this lesson you will be able to:

↗ describe syntax and error messages

↗ duplicate and delete code blocks.

⌘ Learn about...

Every programming language has rules. The rules are the **syntax** of the language. If you write an instruction with the wrong syntax it will not work. The computer will not be able to understand the instruction. This is called a **syntax error**.

Every programmer makes errors sometimes. If you make errors it does not mean you are bad at programming. The key to good programming is to spot the errors, then fix them. If you can do this you can be a good programmer.

Error messages

The computer may spot a syntax error in your program. The computer will show an error message or warning. The message should tell you where the error is and how you can fix it. Look out for error messages as you complete this task.

⏻ How to...

You have learned how to add buttons to the interface. Now you will add an extra button. The new button is called a Reset button. When the user clicks this button the text of `NameLabel` will go back to blank.

↗ **Add a new button to the interface. Name the button** `ResetButton`. **Make the text property** `Reset`

↗ **Go to the Blocks screen. Look in the menu on the left. Find** `ResetButton` **and click it. You will see many blocks that belong with** `ResetButton`. **Find the block that says** `when ResetButton.Click`

↗ **Drag this block onto the Designer section of the screen. This block will be triggered when the user clicks** `ResetButton`

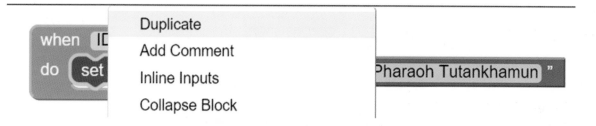

when IDButton ▾ **.Click**
do set NameLabel ▾ . Text ▾ to " Pharaoh Tutankhamun "

when ResetButton ▾ **.Click**
do

If you can't remember how to do these things, look back at Lesson 2.1 or 2.2.

Duplicate blocks

In Lesson 2.2 you made a block of code that set the text of `NameLabel`. Now you will make a copy of this block of code. You can make a small change to the copy so that it sets the text to a blank.

↗ **Look at the code blocks you have already made. Find the block that sets the text of** `NameLabel`

↗ **Right-click this block. That means click the block with the right button of the mouse**

↗ **A menu appears. Choose Duplicate from the menu**

when ID
do set

| Duplicate |
| Add Comment |
| Inline Inputs |
| Collapse Block |

Pharaoh Tutankhamun "

You have made an exact copy of the program block.

↗ **Drag the Duplicate block down to the** `ResetButton` **block.**
The Duplicate block will fit exactly into the new place

↗ **Delete your name so the Text block is empty**

The blocks mean 'When the user clicks ResetButton, set the text property of NameLabel to blank.' The program is ready.

when ResetButton ▾ **.Click**
do set NameLabel ▾ . Text ▾ to " "

Delete blocks

Can you see the rubbish bin at the bottom right of the screen? Sometimes you may accidentally make a block you don't want. You can drag any unwanted block into the rubbish bin. That will delete the block from the screen.

Syntax errors

Commands in App Inventor are held as blocks. The blocks look like jigsaw pieces. If you try to connect the blocks in the wrong order, then they will not join up. Here is an example. These blocks are the wrong way round. They won't fit together.

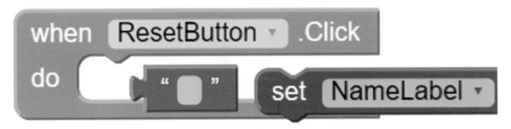

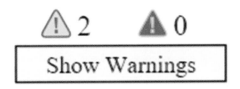

Below these blocks you can see a warning message. There is an exclamation mark in a yellow triangle. A number 2 next to it tells you there are two warnings.

> ↗ **Put the blocks the wrong way round to see this error**
> ↗ **Click Show Warnings**

Exclamation marks appear on the blocks that are the wrong way round. If you click an exclamation mark you will see a message explaining the problem.

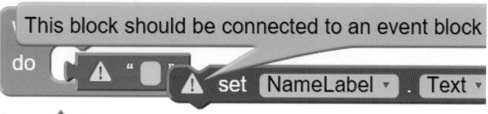

⚠ 2   ⚠ 0

Hide Warnings

⊕ Now you do it...

1 Create a Reset button for the app. Be aware of warning messages and syntax errors as you make the code.

2 Run your app to check it works.

🌐 If you have time...

↗ Change the properties of the Reset button, such as colour and size.

↗ Change the code so that when you press the Reset button the text STAND BY is displayed.

📝 Test yourself...

1 What is program syntax?

2 'A good programmer never makes errors.' Discuss this statement—is it true?

3 Explain how error messages and warning messages may help programmers do their job.

4 Explain how duplicating or copying a block of code may help programmers do their job.

Key words

Right-click: Click the right button of your mouse instead of the left button.

Syntax: The rules of a programming language are called syntax.

Syntax error: A syntax error is when the code breaks the rules of the programming language.

2.4 Display an image

Learning outcomes

You have created a simple app that displays your ID as text. In this lesson you will adapt the app so it also shows a photo of your face. This will help confirm your ID.

When you have completed this lesson you will be able to:

↗ upload and use multimedia content.

⌘ Learn about...

Modern apps use **multimedia** content. That means images, sound and video. Multimedia content makes an app more interesting and enjoyable for the user. There are many ways to make or get multimedia content. For example, you can take a photo with a modern mobile phone. You can also record sound and video clips.

Prepare an image

Take a photo of yourself with a mobile phone, or ask a friend to do it. Transfer the photo to your computer. You could also find an image file on the Internet and make a copy on your computer.

⏻ How to...

When you upload the image file, you will first **upload** the image ready to use.

Look at the Designer screen of App Inventor. At the bottom of the Components section is a small area for Media files.

↗ **Click the button that says Upload File...**
↗ **Click Browse and find the image file you want to use (the photo of you)**
↗ **Click OK to upload it**

Now look in the Media section. You will see the file you uploaded. The image is ready to use in your app. We chose a picture of Tutankhamun.

Add an image object to the screen

Now you will add an image object to the interface. This object will display an image on the interface.

↗ **Look in the Palette. Find the object called Image and drag it onto the screen**

The image object appears on the interface. The image object looks like a little green block. This green block is just a marker to show you where the image will be—you won't see the image yet. We have put the green block above the Reset button. The image object is called Image1.

Set object properties

You can change the properties of Image1. First link it to your picture.

↗ **Select the image object**
↗ **Look at the Properties section of the screen. Find the property called Picture**
↗ **Click this property. You will see a list of uploaded images. Pick the name of your picture**

Make Image1 invisible for now.

↗ **Find the property called Visible. The Visible property is a box with a tick**
↗ **Untick this box**

This image shows the Properties of Image1. The Visible property can be 'true' (ticked) or 'false' (unticked). At the moment the box is unticked. The Visible property is 'false'.

Add code blocks

You made Image1 invisible. Now you can add code that makes Image1 visible. The image will become visible when the user clicks `IDButton`.

↗ **Open the Blocks screen**
↗ **Select the component** `Image1`
↗ **Find the block that says** `set Image1.Visible`

Put this block into the `IDButton` code. The block will fit exactly, like a jigsaw piece.

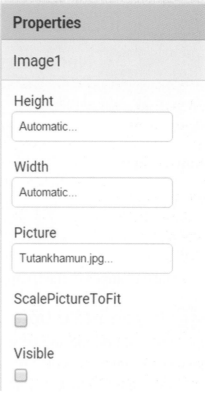

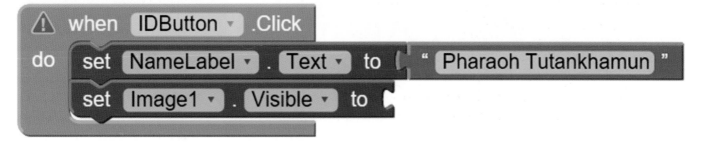

Can you see the red warning symbol on this block? That tells you the task is not finished yet.

We have to set the Visible property to 'true' or 'false'. We want to make `Image1` visible, so we will set the Visible property to 'true'.

↗ **Look in the Blocks section. Find the green Logic category. Click to see Logic blocks**

↗ **The first block is called `true`. Drag this block onto the screen**

↗ **Fit the blocks together as shown here**

These blocks mean 'When the user clicks IDButton, make Object1 visible.' The program is ready.

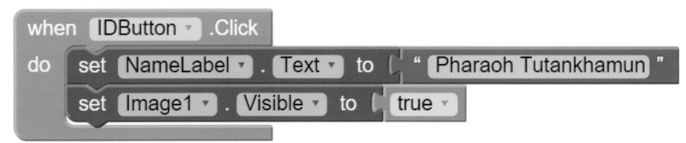

Run the app

↗ **Run the app by clicking `IDButton`**

↗ **You should see your picture on the screen**

 Now you do it...

↗ Make changes to the ID app so that it displays your picture.

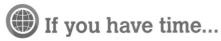 If you have time...

Edit the Reset button so that when the user clicks this button, the picture becomes invisible.

1 Duplicate the block that makes Image1 visible.

2 Fit the duplicate into the `ResetButton` block.

3 Change the value from `true` to `false`. There is a little menu you can use.

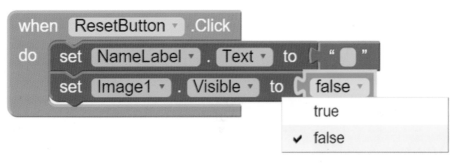

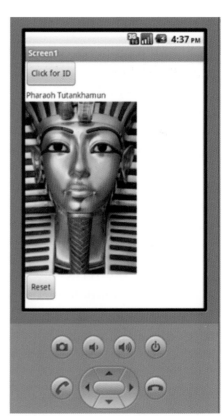

 **Test yourself...**

1   What is the event that makes the image visible?

2   What is the advantage of showing an image on an ID card? What else could you include on an ID card?

3   You added an image object to the interface. What is the purpose of this object?

4   You changed two properties of the image object. Why did you have to change these properties?

FACT

Multimedia

Multimedia content can be stored using many different formats. The name of the multimedia file ends with a three- or four-letter code that tells you the format. For example, .jpeg and .gif are image formats; .wav and .mp3 are audio formats.

Key words

Multimedia: Multimedia content means images, sound and video.

Upload: When a file is uploaded, it is copied onto a computer that is connected to the Internet. The file can be accessed and used over the Internet.

Learning outcomes

You have created a simple app that displays your name and photo when you press a button. In this lesson you will adapt the app by adding a password. The ID card app will only work if you know the right password.

When you have completed this lesson you will be able to:

↗ design an interface with text boxes

↗ use logical tests and the `if` command to control the computer.

⌘ Learn about...

In this lesson you will change the program. The user will enter a password. The app will test to see whether the password is right. If it is right, the app will show the name and photo.

Logical test

This is an example of selection. You learned about the idea of selection in Chapter 1, Computational thinking. Selection is an important part of programming. In this lesson you will use selection with App Inventor.

A programmer often wants to make a computer carry out a test and then make a choice. For example, a programmer wants to write a program to control a self-driving car. Here are some things the program has to do.

↗ If the driver enters the right passcode, the car will start.

↗ If the sensor detects an object ahead, the car will steer around it.

↗ If the speed is too great, the car will slow down.

Each example starts with the word `if`. Then there is a **logical test**. A logical test means a test which only has two possible results:

↗ 'true'

↗ 'false'.

For example, either there is an object ahead (the result of the test is 'true') or there isn't (the result of the test is 'false').

Equals

The logical test you will make in this lesson uses the equals sign. The result of the text is 'true' if the two values on either side of the equals sign are the same. There are other types of logical test and you will learn about them in later chapters.

How to...

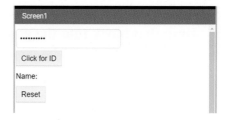

You can add a new object to the interface. The new object is a text box. That is a space on the interface where the user can type input. The user will enter the password into this box.

Look in the Palette. You will see there is a special kind of text box called a PasswordTextBox. The PasswordTextBox is a text box that shows *** instead of the letters you type. No one can read your password over your shoulder.

↗ **Drag the Password text box onto the interface**

Make a logical test

Now you can make the computer test the password. Remember you must start with the word `if`. There is a special block for that.

↗ **Open the Blocks screen**
↗ **Find the yellow/brown Control blocks**
↗ **The first block in this section is the `if` block. Drag it onto the Viewer**

Now you need to add a logical test. The test will use the equals sign (=). The equals sign compares two values. If the two values are equal the result of the test is 'true'.

↗ **Find the green Logic blocks**
↗ **One of the blocks in that section is the equals block**
↗ **Slot the equals block into the `if` block. The equals block fits exactly**

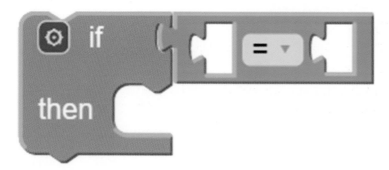

Now you have to tell the computer what two values to compare. There are two gaps in the equals block. You will put two different values into those two gaps. If the two values match then the result of the test is 'true'.

On one side put the password text. That is the text entered by the user into the password box.

↗ **Look at the list of blocks on the left of the screen**
↗ **Click the object `PasswordTextBox1` to find the blocks that go with this object**

↗ **Find the block that says** `PasswordTextBox1.Text`

↗ **Drag that block into the gap in the** = **box**

On the other side type the right password.

↗ **Find the pink Text blocks**

↗ **Drag an empty text box into the other gap in the** = **box**

↗ **Type the word in the empty text box that you want to be the password**

The finished logical test will look something like this:

We have used the password `KingBC`. You can use any password you like.

If the result of the test is 'true'

If the result is 'true', the computer will show your name and photo.

↗ **Take the name and image blocks out of the** `IDButton` **block and put them into the** `if` **block**

Now you can fit it all back together.

↗ **Put the** `if` **block back into the** `IDButton` **block**

The completed program looks like this:

This is what these blocks mean: 'When the user clicks the ID button, if the password is right, then show the name and photo.' That is the right instruction.

↗ **Run the app to check that the program works**

⊕ Now you do it...

↗ Add password protection to your app by adding a password box to the interface. Use the `if` block to make the computer check the password text. You can choose any password you like.

🌐 If you have time...

↗ Here is a short extra task to test your skills. Add a new block to the Reset button. When the user clicks the Reset button the password box will reset to blank.

↗ Here is a longer task if you have made good progress. Add an extra button to the app. If the user clicks on the new button a different name and face will appear on the screen. Now the ID app can be used by two people. You will have to do a lot of work to make this happen, but it is good practice in using your programming skills.

📋 Test yourself...

1 When you type letters into a password text box, the letters do not appear on the screen. Instead you see this symbol *. Why is that?

2 A logical test only has two possible answers. What are they?

3 In this lesson there are three examples of tests that might be needed by software that runs a self-drive car. Think of some more tests that might be needed by this software.

4 Describe the logical test you used in this lesson. When is the result of the test 'true'?

F|A|C|T

Common passwords

Some passwords are very common. Lots of people use these passwords. The most common passwords are '123456', 'qwerty' and 'password'. Do not use passwords like these. That makes it easy for other people to guess your password.

Talk about...

Some passwords are easy to guess, and some are much harder. What makes a password easy to guess? What makes a good password?

Key words

Logical test: A logical test compares two values. The result of the test can be either 'true' or 'false'. In this lesson you saw a logical test that uses the equals sign. There are other types of logical test.

Learning outcomes

You have made a simple app which shows an ID card on the screen of the computer.

When you have completed this lesson you will be able to:

↗ test and evaluate a program to see whether it meets user needs.

⌘ Learn about...

Every app is made for a purpose.

↗ Sometimes a programmer works for a **client**. The client pays the programmer. The client tells the programmer what the app should do.

↗ Sometimes the programmer makes an app to sell to customers. The customers will buy the app if it is useful to them.

In both cases the app has to be useful. The app has to do what the client or the customers want. Otherwise, no one will pay for the app.

When you have made an app you must **evaluate** it. This means checking that the app does what the client wants. If the app passes the evaluation, it is ready for the client.

The output of the program is what the client will see when running the app. When we evaluate a program we evaluate the output. The output should match what the client wants.

Testing

The programmer has to make sure an app produces the right outputs. The programmer will test the app. Testing involves input and output.

↗ Type input into the app. The input is called test data.

↗ See what the output is. The output is called test results.

If the test results do not match the client's requirements then the programmer must make corrections. Then the programmer will test the app again. When the test results match the client's requirements, the app is ready. The programmer can give the app to the client.

The software development process

This diagram represents the process of developing software.

Get the client's requirements → Make the app → Test the app → Compare test results to requirements → If results match requirements, app is ready

Extension and improvement

If the app meets the client's requirements it is completed and no more work is needed. However, sometimes the programmer will think of other improvements. The programmer will add extra features to the app to make it even better.

 How to...

There are two buttons on the app: `IDButton` and `ResetButton`. There is one other input on the app: the password. You can test all these inputs. Try these tests.

↗ **Type the right password and click** `IDButton`

↗ **Click** `ResetButton`

↗ **Type the wrong password and click** `IDButton`

↗ **Don't type a password at all and click** `IDButton`

Here is the test plan. 'Test Data' is what we will type. 'Expected Result' is what we should see if the app is working correctly. The last two columns are blank for now.

Test	Test	Test Data	Expected Result	Actual Result	Analysis
1	IDButton and right password	KingBC	Name and photo appear		
2	Click ResetButton		Name and photo disappear		
3	IDButton and wrong password	12345	No name or photo		
4	IDButton and no password		No name or photo		

↗ **Open a document and make this table**

Carry out tests

Now you will carry out the tests.

↗ **Run the app**

↗ **Carry out the first test. Input the test data**

↗ **Record the output in the Actual Result column**

↗ **Repeat for all the tests**

Analyse test results

Finally, compare the actual results and the expected results. If they match, the program is working correctly. If they do not match, the program must be improved. This is called analysis of test results.

↗ **Write the analysis of test results in the final column of the table**

Test	Test	Test Data	Expected Result	Actual Result	Analysis
1	IDButton and right password	KingBC	Name and photo appear	Name and photo appear	Passes the test
2	Click ResetButton		Name and photo disappear	Name and photo disappear	Passes the test
3	IDButton and wrong password	12345	No name or photo	No name or photo	Passes the test
4	IDButton and no password		No name or photo	No name or photo	Passes the test

If the actual and expected results do not match, you have found an error in the program. You must correct the error.

Finished program

Here is the completed program with all blocks in place.

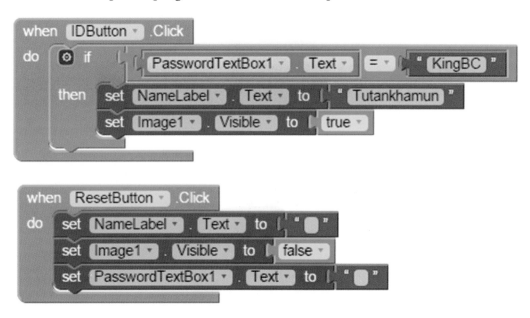

⊕ Now you do it...

1 Test the app you have made.

2 Record the results in a test table.

3 Analyse the test results.

🌐 If you have time...

↗ In Lessons 2.3 and 2.4 you added extra features to the app. Extend your test plan to test these extra features.

↗ Think about more features you could add to the app. If you have time, add more features to extend and improve the app.

 Test yourself...

1   Why does a programmer evaluate a program?

2   What are test data?

3   A programmer made a test plan. One column of the plan was called 'Expected Result'. What goes in that column?

4   A programmer tested an app. Analysis of test results showed that the programmer had more work to do before the app was ready. Explain why.

Talk about...

What makes a good ID card app? What extra features could you add to this app to make it better?

FACT

How many apps are there?

In July 2015, about 1.6 million apps were available for use on Android phones. Apple's App Store offered users 1.5 million apps. These numbers are increasing all the time.

Key words

Client: The client is the person who pays for the app. The client has requirements. The output of the program must match the client's requirements.

Evaluate: Compare the output of software to the client's requirements. If the output matches these requirements, then the app is ready to use.

Review what you have learned about App Inventor

Overview

In this chapter you have created a simple app for a mobile phone. The app displays an ID card. The card includes your name and your photo. The ID card is password protected.

You have learned how to:

- ↗ design an interface with buttons, labels and text boxes
- ↗ make an event-driven program that reacts to user commands
- ↗ display text and images as output from a computer program
- ↗ describe syntax and error messages

- ↗ duplicate and delete code blocks
- ↗ upload and use multimedia content
- ↗ use logical tests and the `if` command to control the computer
- ↗ test and evaluate a program to see whether it meets user needs.

Test questions

Answer these questions to check how well you have learned this topic.

1   A touch-screen interface is made up of objects. Describe three objects you can add to a touch-screen interface.

2   The objects on an interface have properties. Describe three properties of interface objects.

3   What is a client?

4   Explain why you must know the client's requirements before you begin making an app.

5   App Inventor is an event-driven visual programming language. Explain what that means.

6   What is a logical test?

7   Explain how the equals sign is used in a logical test.

The next three questions relate to this image. The image shows a block of program code. The code is part of a science quiz.

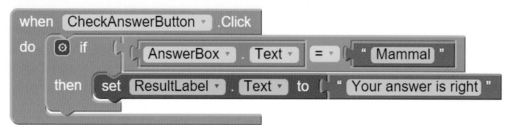

8   What is the logical test in this block of code?

9   What happens if the result of the logical test is 'true'?

10 What event triggers this block of code?

 # Assessment activities

A programmer made an app that shows pictures of famous landmarks. The interface she made is shown below.

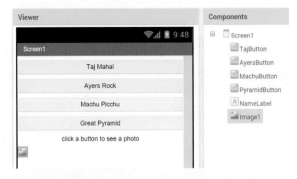

Here is part of the code that makes this app work:

```
when  MachuButton ▾ .Click
do   set  Image1 ▾ . Picture ▾  to (  " Peru.jpg "
     set  NameLabel ▾ . Text ▾  to (  " Machu Picchu is in Peru "
     set  MachuButton ▾ . BackgroundColor ▾  to (  ⬜
```

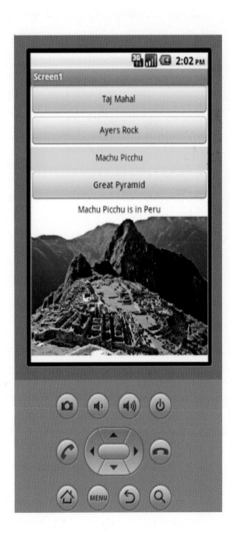

The image on the right shows what the app looks like when it is running.

Starter activity

Make the interface and code that you see on this page.
You will need to:

- ↗ add buttons, labels and images to the interface
- ↗ give names to the objects and change the text
- ↗ find an image of Machu Picchu and upload it
- ↗ make the code that goes with the Machu Picchu button
- ↗ copy what you see on this page.

Intermediate activity

- ↗ Add code to all buttons on the interface. If users click on any button they will see an image of that landmark and its name on the screen.

Extension activity

- ↗ Add password protection and a Reset button to the Famous Landmarks app.
- ↗ Test the app and record the test results.
- ↗ If you have time, add extra features to the app.

Data and the CPU

Sending codes

Computers are everywhere in our lives. Every day we see computers carry out tasks that would have seemed unthinkable even a few years ago. A car that drives itself? Surely, that's impossible!

You may think that computers must be complicated devices to do such tasks.

However, a computer is fundamentally a simple device. It uses a special number system called binary to do everyday tasks. You will learn about binary numbers. You will also learn how to convert numbers between binary and decimal. (Decimal is the number system that we use.) You will find out how computers use codes to convert binary numbers into information that we can understand.

Learning outcomes

By the end of this chapter you will know how to:

- ⬈ explain why computers use binary code
- ⬈ convert decimal numbers into binary
- ⬈ convert binary numbers into decimal
- ⬈ explain how counting works in decimal and binary
- ⬈ explain how computers use binary numbers to store useful information such as text and symbols
- ⬈ explain why a computer needs to use code to communicate
- ⬈ encode and decode simple messages
- ⬈ show that simple programs use variables and constants
- ⬈ explain that data are stored in a data structure.

Talk about...

Computers are everywhere in our lives. You can see computers in almost every school, office and home. You may be familiar with desktop and laptop computers. There are also many more devices that you may not know are computers, but which are controlled by computer technology.

For example, modern mobile phones can run the same type of programs and games as desktop computers. Many other devices in your home have computer technology built in—even washing machines. You will also come across computer technology in shops, on the street and in cars.

Do computers always improve our lives? Can you think of two examples from the past week where a computer has made your life better, easier or just more enjoyable? Can you explain for each example how the computer improved things for you?

Sending code

In this chapter you will send secret messages to others using code. People have used code to send secret messages for centuries. The ancient Romans used a code called the Caesar cipher. In more recent history, during the Second World War, each country had people working to break their enemies' codes. British scientists developed computers at Bletchley Park, Buckinghamshire, in the UK, during the Second World War to speed up their code breaking. Alan Turing helped to develop the Colossus computer and was an important person in the history of computing.

Binary

Number   ASCII code   Digit

Bit

Ones   Clock speed   Zeros   **Byte**

Unicode   Messages   Microprocessor

Binary digit   **Cipher**   Convert

Characters   Cipher

Equivalent

Morse code   Decimal digit

Carry   Languages

Substitute

What is a computer?

Learning outcomes

When you have completed this lesson you will be able to:

⬈ explain why computers use binary code.

⌘ Learn about...

Each minute of every day computers carry out complex tasks. Computers make difficult calculations quickly and can create complex 3D high-resolution game worlds on screen. They can even guide a space probe across the Solar System. Modern computers are complex. Underneath, though, the computer is a simple machine.

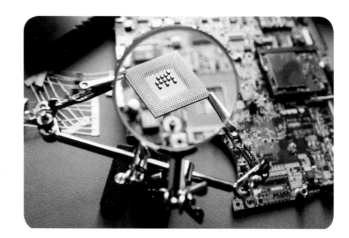

A processor, sometimes called the central processing unit or CPU, is the brain of the computer. The CPU is where all the work is carried out. Computer processors have become more powerful, less expensive and much smaller over time.

A computer processor fits on a single chip of silicon about the size of a fingernail. Modern computer processors are called **microprocessors** because they are so small. (Micro means small.) As processors have reduced in size, so have computers.

The code-breaking Colossus computers were so large that two steel buildings were built at Bletchley Park (in Buckinghamshire, in the UK) to hold just ten of them. Each Colossus computer weighed about as much as a medium-sized car. Compare the size of a Colossus to a laptop trolley in your school, which may hold around 30 computers. Each one of these school computers is many times more powerful than a Colossus.

As microprocessors become smaller and cheaper, we can build them into all sorts of devices. Cars, supermarket checkouts and washing machines are all devices that have microprocessors.

What is inside a microprocessor?

At the centre of the microprocessor is a small chip of silicon about the size of a fingernail. On that chip are tens of millions of tiny components called transistors. A transistor is a type of switch. Like a light switch, a transistor can be either on or off.

A modern computer is made from a mass of connected switches. The combination of switches being turned on and off is what makes the computer work.

Computers carry out complicated tasks because they can work fast. The computer has a clock inside. Each time the clock ticks, an instruction is carried out. It all happens very quickly.

What language does a computer use?

In English, people use an alphabet of 26 letters, 10 numbers (0–9) and other characters, for example the full stop and comma. To communicate we combine letters, numbers and other characters to make words and sentences that others can understand.

The computer processor may work very quickly, but it is a much simpler tool than a human brain. The computer cannot recognise the same number of characters that we can. The computer can only recognise two characters—on and off. To make life simpler, programmers replace on and off with the numbers 1 and 0. These two numbers are the only characters in the computer's language.

We call the computer's language **binary**. Binary is a number system that only uses two digits: 0 and 1.

The computer can combine characters to make words. However, the computer's words will only ever be made up of the digits 0 and 1. The words look like this:

01000100 01100100 01101001 01110101

 **How to...**

How fast does a microprocessor work?

The speed that the CPU processes instructions is given by the speed of its internal clock. We call this the computer's **clock speed**. How quickly can you process instructions?

With a partner, make a copy of these multiplication questions. Time how quickly you can each write the answers. Who was fastest? How many seconds did it take?

1 $4 \times 6 =$
2 $2 \times 9 =$
3 $3 \times 3 =$
4 $10 \times 10 =$
5 $9 \times 8 =$
6 $3 \times 9 =$
7 $7 \times 7 =$
8 $8 \times 5 =$
9 $6 \times 6 =$
10 $8 \times 4 =$

Computer clock speed is measured in hertz (Hz). Hz means number of times per second. A clock with a speed of 1000 Hz ticks 1000 times every second. If you answered the 10 questions in 20 seconds, how many instructions did you follow in one second?

The answer is 10 instructions divided by 20 seconds = 0.5 Hz. You carried out half an instruction in one second.

 Work out your clock speed based on the task you carried out.

A normal home computer has a clock speed of 2.5 gigahertz (GHz). Giga means one thousand million. So, a clock speed of 2.5 GHz means the computer's clock ticks 2,500,000,000 times per second. Each time the clock ticks, the computer carries out an instruction. Compare this to the speed at which you completed the multiplication task. A computer works very quickly.

⊕ Now you do it...

Microprocessors are all around the home. You don't just find them in computers. Microprocessors are in any device that has automatic controls. We know that a modern washing machine has a microprocessor. Make a list of other devices in the home that contain microprocessors.

You could work in groups and challenge each other to see who can make the longest list.

🌐 If you have time...

You know that a modern washing machine contains microprocessors. Make a list of the things you think a microprocessor controls in a washing machine.

If you have access to the Internet, you could carry out some research. Use a search such as:

> microprocessors in washing machines

📄 Test yourself...

1 What is the language used by computers called?
2 What does 'micro' in microprocessor mean?
3 Why does a computer have a clock?
4 What does 'giga' in gigahertz mean?

FACT

Microprocessors

A modern car contains around 50 microprocessors that are responsible for the performance, safety and comfort of the car. Microprocessors manage the climate control system, making sure passengers are not too hot or too cold. Microprocessors also control the satellite navigation system that helps the driver reach a destination, and they control the braking system and other safety features, such as airbags. One of the most important functions of the car's microprocessors is to manage the engine to minimise environmental impact.

Key words

Binary: Binary is a number system that only uses the digits 0 and 1.

Clock speed: The clock speed is the speed at which a computer's internal clock ticks. Each time the clock ticks, the computer carries out an instruction. A computer clock ticks millions of times every second.

Microprocessor: The microprocessor is the brain of a computer. A microprocessor is about the size of a fingernail.

What is a byte?

Learning outcomes

When you have completed this lesson you will be able to:

↗ convert binary numbers into decimal.

⌘ Learn about...

Remember that the number system we use every day is called the decimal system. We write numbers using the **decimal digits** 0, 1, 2, 3, 4, 5, 6, 7, 8 and 9. Some people think the decimal system came about because we started to count with our ten fingers.

You have learned that a computer uses a different number system called binary. Binary only uses two digits: 0 and 1.

Decimal numbers

What does the number 2382 mean?

We use decimal numbers so often that we rarely stop to think what they mean. One way to describe a number is to write it into a value table like this:

Thousands	Hundreds	Tens	Units
2	3	8	2

The number 2382 has been split up into four separate decimal digits. A decimal digit is a single digit between 0 and 9. You can write the value of each digit in the number 2382 by multiplying the digit by the value of its column.

Now we can describe the number 2382 as:

(two thousands = 2000) + (three hundreds = 300) + (eight tens = 80) + (2 units) = 2382

Base 10

The decimal number system is sometimes called base 10. Base 10 is a useful way to describe a number system because it tells us two things.

↗ There are ten digits in the system: 0, 1, 2, 3, 4, 5, 6, 7, 8, 9.
↗ As you move from right to left, the value of each column is ten times greater than the previous one.

Reading binary numbers

We call the decimal system base 10. In the same way, the binary system is called base 2. A base-2 system means two things.

↗ There are two digits in the system: 0 and 1.
↗ As you move from right to left, the value of each column is two times greater than the previous one.

Here is a binary number:

1101

We can describe this binary number by putting it in a value table, just like a decimal number.

8s	4s	2s	Units
1	1	0	1

The value of the columns does not increase by ten times from right to left as values do in the base-10 system. In binary (or base 2) the value of the columns increases by two times. The column value doubles.

We can describe the binary number 1101 as:

↗ (1 eight = 8) + (1 four = 4) + (0 twos = 0) + (1 unit = 1) = 13
↗ 1101 in binary = 8 + 4 + 0 + 1 = 13

⏻ How to...

You can practise converting binary numbers into decimal numbers in this simple game.

1 Work with a partner to each choose a four-digit binary number and write it on a slip of paper.

2 Swap the slips of paper.

3 Now the race is on. Calculate the decimal value of the binary number your partner gave you and write it next to the binary number.

4 Check the answer with your partner. The winner is the person who wrote the correct decimal number first.

5 Play three rounds of this game. With practice you will get faster and better at calculating the right answer.

Bits and bytes

You have learned that the binary number system uses just two digits: 0 and 1. A single **binary digit** is called a **bit**. The word bit is formed from the start and end of the term 'binary digit'.

A single binary digit does not hold enough information to be useful on its own, so binary digits are grouped into blocks of eight.

A group of eight bits is called a **byte**. A byte looks like this:

01001001

You always use all eight bits in a byte even if it means starting the number with some zeros.

Convert a byte to decimal

You know how to convert a four-bit binary number into a decimal. You can convert a byte into a decimal value in exactly the same way. You just need to make the table bigger to include eight bits, instead of four.

Remember, the value of each column doubles as you move from right to left.

Convert the byte 01001001.

	×2	×2	×2	×2	×2	×2	×2
128s	64s	32s	16s	8s	4s	2s	Units
0	1	0	0	1	0	0	1

To make your calculations simpler, you can ignore the zeros in the byte. Zero multiplied by anything is always zero. Just add together the value of those columns with the number 1 in them.

$64 + 8 + 1 = 73$

The byte 01001001 is 73 in decimal.

Repeat the game you played before, but this time challenge your partner to convert a byte instead of a four-bit binary number.

The byte you pass to your partner must contain eight bits.

Play as many rounds as you can. The more you practise converting binary numbers, the easier it will get.

⊕ Now you do it...

1   Work with a partner to each draw up a copy of the following table. Think of three eight-digit binary numbers (bytes) and enter the three bytes into the table.

2   Work out the decimal number represented by each byte so you can check your partner's answers later.

3   Swap grids. Work out the decimal number for each of your partner's three bytes. The first person to convert all three bytes into decimal correctly is the winner.

128	64	32	16	8	4	2	Units

If you have time...

You wake up one morning to find an alien spaceship has crashed in your garden. An alien is standing by the wrecked ship so you introduce yourself. You exchange names and somehow you manage to ask her age using sign language. She holds up fingers to show she is 125. You are surprised—she looks much younger.

You notice that the alien only has three fingers on each hand. Remembering that some people think we use a base-10 system based on our ten fingers you wonder if the aliens use a base-6 system for the same reason.

If you are right, how old is the alien in decimal years? Use this table to help you work it out.

?	?	Units
1	2	5

 Test yourself...

1 Convert the binary value 1101 into a decimal.
2 What is each of the digits in a byte called?
3 How would you write 100111 as a byte?
4 What is the largest number that can be stored in a byte? Give your answer in binary and decimal.

Key words

Bit: A bit is a single binary digit.

Binary digit: A binary digit is a digit in the binary number system (also called base 2). In the binary number system, the only digits are 0 and 1.

Byte: A byte is the name for eight bits together, for example 01011100.

Decimal digit: Decimal (or base 10) digits are the numbers we use every day. They are: 0, 1, 2, 3, 4, 5, 6, 7, 8 and 9.

3.3 From decimal to binary

Learning outcomes

When you have completed this lesson you will be able to:

↗ convert decimal numbers into binary

↗ explain how computers use binary numbers.

⌘ Learn about...

So far in this chapter you have learned that the computer uses a different number system from the one we use. The computer processor can output information that we can read, but you can translate binary into decimal yourself. You learned in Lesson 3.2 how to convert a binary number to decimal. In this lesson you will learn how to convert a decimal number to binary.

⏻ How to...

What does the decimal number 85 look like in binary?

The first step in converting the number is to draw up a byte table. The values at the top of the table show the value of a 1 in that column. Each value increases by two times as you move through each column from right to left.

128	64	32	16	8	4	2	1

1   Take the decimal number you want to convert. In this case the decimal number is 85. Then **working from left to right** find the first column heading that is smaller than 85. Write a 1 in that column. In this case the column is 64.

2   Subtract 64 from your original number 85.

    85 − 64 = 21

3   Repeat the process using the remainder (21).

4   Keep repeating until you are left with a remainder of 0.

5   When you have finished enter 0 into any blank cells.

This is how you will record your work using the byte table.

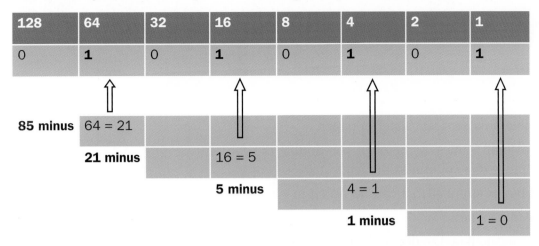

128	64	32	16	8	4	2	1
0	1	0	1	0	1	0	1

85 minus	64 = 21						
	21 minus		16 = 5				
			5 minus		4 = 1		
					1 minus		1 = 0

Practise converting decimal numbers into binary in this simple game.

1 Work with a partner. Each choose a decimal number between 1 and 255.

2 Write the decimal number on a slip of paper.

3 Swap the slips of paper.

4 Now the race is on. Calculate the binary value of the decimal number your partner gave you and write it next to the decimal number.

5 Check the answer with your partner. The winner is the person who wrote the correct decimal number first.

6 Play three rounds of this game, if you have time. With practice you will get faster and better at calculating the right answer.

How big is a byte?

You learned in Lesson 3.2 that a byte is eight bits long. A byte is more useful than an individual bit because it can be used to store larger numbers in binary. However, even a byte has a limit.

What is the biggest number a byte can hold?

A byte contains the largest number it can hold when every bit is set to 1.

128	64	32	16	8	4	2	1
1	1	1	1	1	1	1	1

If we convert the binary number **11111111** to a decimal number, we get **255**. That is:

$$128 + 64 + 32 + 16 + 8 + 4 + 2 + 1 = 255$$

Storing larger binary numbers

The number 255 isn't very large. There are many times when we need to store larger numbers than 255. For example, there are 365 days in a year, most computers cost more than $255 and it is 3459 miles from London to New York.

When a computer needs to store larger numbers it uses two bytes, or more if necessary. A two-byte number has 16 digits available to store a number. You just keep doubling the value of the column as you move from right to left.

			×2	×2	×2										
?	?	?	?	2048	1024	512	256	128	64	32	16	8	4	2	1
								1	1	1	1	1	1	1	1
Byte 2								**Byte 1**							

1   Draw the two-byte table on a separate sheet of paper.

2   Fill in all the empty column values. Remember, you double the column value each time you move one column to the left.

3   Work out the largest binary number that can be stored in two bytes.

4   What is that number in decimal?

Hint: There is a shortcut to calculate the decimal value of a binary number that only contains 1s. Take the value of the left-hand column. This is the highest value column. Multiply it by 2 and subtract 1.

For example, take the binary number 111:

↗   The highest column value is 4

↗ $4 \times 2 = 8$

↗ $8 - 1 = 7$

⊕ Now you do it...

128	64	32	16	8	4	2	Units

1   Draw this table on a separate sheet of paper, then use it to convert these decimal numbers into binary:

↗   79

↗   138

↗   225

2   Keep a record of your work so you can check where you went wrong if you make a mistake.

3   Check your answers by converting the binary numbers in your table back into decimal.

🌐 If you have time...

Draw a two-byte table like the one you did earlier. Use it to help you convert these decimal values to binary:

↗   255

↗   1455

↗   5100

Test yourself...

1 What would 0 look like if written as a byte?

2 How many bits are there in two bytes?

3 The largest decimal number that can be stored in two bytes is 65,535. What would you do to store a larger number than that?

4 How can you tell whether a binary number is odd or even?

3.4 **Counting in binary**

Learning outcomes

When you have completed this lesson you will be able to:

↗ explain how counting works in decimal and binary.

⌘ Learn about...

You have learned that the binary or base-2 system only uses two digits, 0 and 1. You can now convert from binary to decimal and from decimal to binary.

Counting in binary is just the same as counting in decimal. It is worth thinking about how you count in decimal before moving on to binary because decimal is so familiar.

A simple way to think of counting is that each step in a count is adding 1 to a number. When you think of it like that, counting sounds easy whether you are counting in decimal or binary.

⏻ How to...

There are ten digits in the decimal system with 9 being the highest value.

Counting from 0 to 9 is straightforward. You simply move through the ten digits in order of value; 0-1-2-3-4-5-6-7-8-9.

When you reach 9 you have run out of digits and need to do something different.

Hundreds	Tens	Units
0	0	9

You set the value of the units column back to 0. Next, you carry 1 over into the next column to add to the value already there. **Carry** is when a digit is carried forward from one column to the next during a count. You carry the digit because the lower value column has reached its limit.

This is the result:

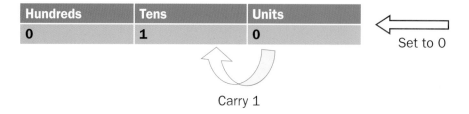

Hundreds	Tens	Units
0	1	0

Set to 0

Carry 1

Sometimes a carry forward will cause another carry. Carrying forward happens a lot in binary, so it is worth thinking about what happens in decimal. You have reached 99 in your count. What happens next?

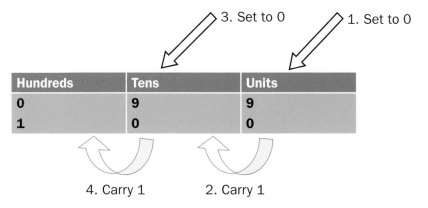

Hundreds	Tens	Units
0	9	9
1	0	0

4. Carry 1   2. Carry 1

✐ Copy the table for counting from 99 to 100 on a separate sheet. Add this title: 'Counting in decimal—what happens when you get to 99'.

✐ Under the table add bullet points that describe what is happening at each of the labels 1 to 4.

Counting in binary

Counting in binary follows exactly the same rules as counting in decimal. There are two things that might make you *think* it is different or more difficult.

1 You have to reset columns to 0 and carry forward more often in binary.

2 There are no names for binary numbers. For example, we have thirteen and fourteen in decimal.

Starting from 0

128	64	32	16	8	4	2	1
0	0	0	0	0	0	0	0

Count 1: We do not go over the highest digit value so no carry is required and we stop.

128	64	32	16	8	4	2	1
0	0	0	0	0	0	0	1

Count 2: This time we do go over the highest digit value (1) so we have to set column one to 0 and carry.

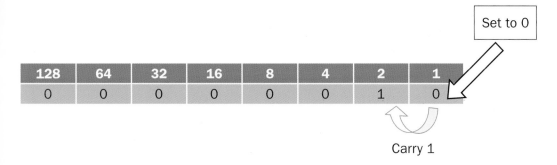

128	64	32	16	8	4	2	1
0	0	0	0	0	0	1	0

Carry 1

Count 3: We do not go over the highest digit value in column one so no carry is required and we stop.

128	64	32	16	8	4	2	1
0	0	0	0	0	0	1	1

Count 4: We have to set column one to 0 and carry into column two. We have had to repeat the same action for columns two and three.

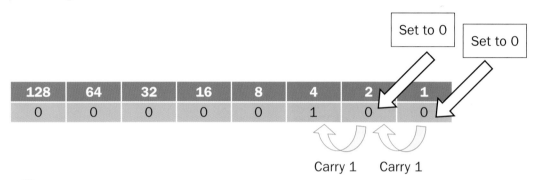

Now you do it...

In this activity you are going to make a simple binary counting machine using four squares of paper. When you have built your machine, you will test it counting from 000 to 111.

1   Cut out four small squares of paper and write '0' on the front and '1' on the back of three of the squares. Draw an arrow on the fourth square.

2   Lay the squares like this:

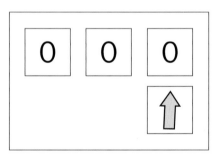

3   On a separate sheet of paper, list the numbers 1–7. Now you will count from 1–7 and record each binary number you count using the square pieces of paper in front of you. Follow these rules.

   a   Turn over the piece of paper that the arrow is pointing to.

   b   If the number changes from a 0 to a 1 then STOP and move the arrow back to its starting position on the right. Write the binary number in front of you in your list.

   c   If the number changes from a 1 to a 0 move the arrow one position to the left.

   d   Repeat the instructions from 1 until you STOP at step 2 then move on to the next number.

To check your answers convert each of the binary numbers back to decimal.

If you have time...

Think back over the chapter so far. Make sure you understand why binary has only two digits. Are you confident converting binary to decimal and decimal to binary? Can you count in binary? If there are any areas you are not feeling very confident about, take some time to look at the relevant lesson again.

 # Test yourself...

1   When do you know a single count (e.g. from 00000111 to 00001000) is completed?

2   If you count one step from 0000001, what happens in the units column?

3   Why do you carry more often in binary than in decimal?

4   Why don't you use words such as 'seven', 'eight' and 'nine' when you count in binary?

Key word

Carry: Carry is when a digit is carried forward from one column to the next during a count. You carry the digit because the lower value column has reached its limit.

Learning outcomes

When you have completed this lesson you will be able to:

- explain why a computer needs to use code to communicate
- encode and decode simple messages.

 Learn about...

People have used codes for many centuries. They use codes to keep information secret. A code is created to change everyday language into words that are meaningless to most people. Only someone who knows what rules were used to create the code can read the message.

Computers use codes too but for a different reason. You have learned that computers use a number system as their language. That number system is called binary or base 2 and it contains only the digits 0 and 1. People use letters and words to communicate and make sense of the world around them. Computers use binary digits and bytes.

For computers and people to understand each other, each has to break the other's code. Each has to understand the rules of the code to communicate.

Millions of people around the world use computers, at home, at school and at work. You probably use a computer every day to do your school work, keep in touch with friends and play games. However, you do not need to type binary messages into a computer or read binary on screen. Even the most dedicated computer specialists avoid binary as much as possible.

All the coding and decoding that needs to be done to translate between computer and human language is carried out automatically. When you press a key on your keyboard, the letter you type is converted into binary automatically. When a word is sent by the computer to your screen it does not arrive in binary. It is automatically translated.

In this lesson you will learn about how to use codes and why codes are so important in computing.

Using codes

Codes have been used for hundreds of years to help us communicate. You can use some codes to hide the contents of messages you want to keep secret. Substitution codes are where letters or numbers are substituted for other ones. A famous substitution code is called the Caesar cipher. **Cipher** is another name for code. Cipher usually refers to a code that is designed for sending secret messages.

We use other types of codes to send messages over long distances using the Internet or other methods where the message has to be converted into electrical signals.

The common feature of all codes is that they have to be translated to make sense of the message. That means that both the person coding a message and the person decoding the message have to understand the rules of the code.

The Romans used the Caesar cipher many centuries ago. The Caesar cipher works by shifting the letters three steps along the alphabet.

The letter A shifts three letters to become D.

B → E

C → F

D → G

E → H

and so on.

So, in Caesar cipher the word BAD is now written as: EDG

Julius Caesar never varied his simple code. You can improve the Caesar code by introducing a key. The key to the code is the number of letters to shift along the alphabet. For example, if the key to the cipher is five, then you move along the alphabet by five letters. You can vary your code each time you use it by changing the key. Changing the key keeps your enemies guessing. If only Julius Caesar had thought of this the Roman army might rule the world today!

 How to...

You can learn how to write messages in code. Work with a partner to practise your knowledge of code keys. Decide on your code key—that is, how many places you will shift the alphabet along. For example, if your code key is five, then A → F and so on.

1   To create your code, write the alphabet down the side of a piece of paper. Write the substitute letters beside the original alphabetical list.

2   Write a short message to your partner using the code.

3   Pass the message and the key to your partner to decode.

How did your partner work out the code? Can you think of any ways you could make the code more difficult to decode?

Morse code

Morse code was invented by Samuel Morse in 1836. Morse developed the code around the time that the first electrical telegraph was invented. The telegraph sent messages using pulses of electricity along wires. Morse developed his code as a way of sending messages by the new electrical telegraph. Morse code consists of only two 'digits', short signals called dots and long signals called dashes.

Can you see the similarities between Morse code and the way computers use binary to communicate?

Morse code was not invented as a way of sending secret messages. It was designed as a code that everyone could share. Morse intended that people should be able to understand a telegraph message wherever they were in the world. He was successful and the international distress call 'SOS' is still recognised across the world by its Morse code. Technology has moved on and Morse code has not been used officially since 1999.

.	.	.	–	–	–	.	.	.
dot	dot	dot	dash	dash	dash	dot	dot	dot
S			**O**			**S**		

The telegraph sent Morse code as short and long pulses of electricity along a cable. The pulses were converted into a sound at the other end so they could be understood by a trained operator. Ships could also send Morse code to each other by using short and long bursts of light.

Work with a partner to send a Morse code message by using a torch or by holding up a piece of paper.

↗ Use the Morse code key to write a short message in Morse code.

↗ Send the Morse code message to your partner. You can use a torch, a piece of paper as a flag or agree a method of tapping with your fingers. For example, a tap with a single finger could be a dot and a longer roll with three or four fingers a dash.

↗ Can your partner understand your message?

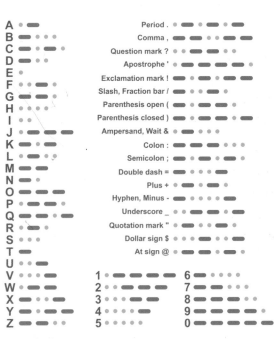

Morse code key

Now you do it...

Work with a partner to invent your own code based on binary numbers.

Letter	Binary code
a	00000000
b	00000001
c	00000010
d	00000011
e	00000100
f	00000101

1   Create a table with two columns like this one. You will need a row for each of the 26 letters in the alphabet. You should also have a code for a space character, a full stop, a comma and a question mark.

2   Use a byte to represent each of the letters in your code. Start with 00000000 to represent 'a' then number each character in your list in order.

3   When you have completed your code, write a question to your partner. Remember to use the space character to separate words. Use the other punctuation marks where you need them. There is no need to write a long question.

4   Your partner can decode your question and send an answer, also in code.

If you have time...

Many other codes have been invented for sending secret messages. Do a web search to discover more about those codes. Start with a search such as:

Secret codes

When you have found a code you like, try it out with a partner. Make notes so that you remember how the code works. You might also want to make notes on why you think your code will be more difficult to work out than the Caesar cipher.

 ## Test yourself...

1   What is the Caesar cipher?

2   Why does a computer need to use codes to communicate with people?

3   Explain how Morse code is similar to binary code.

4   What is a key used for in codes?

Key words

Cipher: Cipher is another name for code. Cipher usually refers to a code that is designed for sending secret messages.

Morse code: Morse code was created in 1836 by Samuel Morse to send messages across the electrical telegraph system. Morse code consists of only two 'digits', short signals called dots and long signals called dashes.

3.6 The codes computers use

Learning outcomes

When you have completed this lesson you will be able to:

↗ explain how computers use binary numbers to store useful information such as text and symbols.

⌘ Learn about...

In Lesson 3.5 you made a code. Using the code, you sent a question to a partner in binary and decoded the answer.

The binary code you used to send a question is almost the same as the binary code computers use. Computers use binary code to process the letters and other characters that make up our language. The code the computer uses is called ASCII (American Standard Code for Information Interchange). ASCII is pronounced Ask-ee. **ASCII code** is a method for representing letters, symbols and numbers as binary data. When you press a key on your keyboard the character is translated into a binary number using the ASCII code. Once a character is converted into binary, the computer can store it and work with it. When a computer wants to send a message to the screen or a printer, the process is reversed. Each character in the message is translated back from a binary number into a character we can read.

That is how we communicate with a computer without wearing out the 0 and 1 keys on our keyboard.

⏻ How to...

ASCII uses a single byte to store characters but it only uses seven bits of each byte. This means that ASCII only has enough binary numbers available to store 128 characters. The bit on the extreme left of each byte is not used and is always set to zero.

128	64	32	16	8	4	2	1
0	1	1	1	1	1	1	1
Not used	7 bits used for ASCII codes						

When you type a message you use a combination of upper-case and lower-case letters. For example, you write 'ASCII' entirely in upper-case letters. You write your name in a mix of upper-case and lower-case letters.

We think of upper-case and lower-case letters as being the same. They have the same meaning to us. The computer sees them as completely different and has to use different ASCII codes for 'A' and 'a'.

Here are the ASCII codes for some of the upper-case and lower-case letters. You can try to work out the rest. Notice that the only difference between upper-case and lower-case ASCII codes is the sixth digit from the right. The digit is 0 for upper-case letters and 1 for lower-case letters.

Letter	ASCII Binary	ASCII Decimal	Letter	ASCII Binary	ASCII Decimal
A	01000001	065	a	01100001	097
B	01000010	066	b	01100010	098
C	01000011	067	c	01100011	099
Z	01011010	090	z	01111010	122

Numbers in ASCII

When a computer needs to communicate a number to us, it uses the number characters 0 to 9. These characters have ASCII codes too. Some are shown in this table. Try to work out the rest.

Number	ASCII Binary	ASCII Decimal
0	00110000	048
1	00110001	049
9	00111001	057

Other characters in ASCII

When you write sentences you need more than just letters and numbers. You also need punctuation and other characters. Here are some of the main characters you will need. It might surprise you that a space needs its own ASCII code.

Character	ASCII Binary	ASCII Decimal	Letter	ASCII Binary	ASCII Decimal
space	00100000	032	.	00101110	046
,	00101100	044	!	00100001	033
?	00111111	063	%	00100101	037

You have learned that once you have a few examples it is possible to work out the ASCII codes for letters and numbers. You can work out the codes because you know the sequence of the alphabet. Punctuation characters do not have a sequence, so you have to look them up in the ASCII table if you want to use them.

Can you think of any other characters that you might need to use when typing at your computer? For example, think about typing an assignment for your maths course.

↗   Make a list of five characters you might need.

↗   Can you find the ASCII codes for those characters?

You can do some research using the Internet to find a list of ASCII codes. You could use this search:

ASCII binary code

What if we need more characters?

ASCII only provides 128 characters. It does not include any characters used by languages other than English. There are hundreds of other written languages in use around the world that ASCII does not provide characters for. That is a problem. There are 1.5 billion people who speak Mandarin or Arabic and many of them want to use computers!

Extended ASCII

Remember that ASCII only uses seven bits in its code. Extended ASCII uses all of the eight bits in a byte. Using that extra bit provides an extra 128 characters. Having the extra characters is good news for users of European languages. In Spain they can use the cedilla (Ç) and in the Czech Republic they can use the caron (Ď). However, there are still not enough characters for speakers of Hindi, Urdu, Mandarin and Arabic.

Unicode

In Lesson 3.4 you learned that computers can handle large numbers by using more than one byte. It is exactly the same with characters. If we use more bytes we can create more characters. **Unicode** is a system that uses up to four bytes to store character codes. Unicode is another method for representing letters, symbols and numbers as binary data. Unicode can manage more characters than ASCII.

In the Unicode system there are over 128,000 characters that support hundreds of languages. Computers can now be used in Arabic, Hindi, Somali and Japanese. In fact, they can be used in about any written language you can think of and lots that you cannot.

If you want to send an email in Norwegian Bokmål, Cornish, Shekhawati, Navajo or Old Norse, go ahead!

 Now you do it...

This message is written in ASCII code. The message only contains characters that are either given to you in this lesson or that you can work out yourself. You can work out the characters yourself by extending the tables of letters and numbers. Can you translate the message? Look out for repeated codes so that you don't have to look them up more than once.

01000010 01101001 01101110 01100001 01110010 01111001 00100000 01101001 01110011
00100000 00110001 00110000 00110000 00100101 00100000 01100110 01110101 01101110
00100001

 If you have time...

You are almost at the end of this chapter. You have learned some important new skills on the way. Here is a short message that you will probably like to include in a text or email to your friends.

00111010 00101101 00101001

You will need to look up the characters in an ASCII table. Find an ASCII table online or your teacher will be able to provide one.

 Test yourself...

1 Why is ASCII code important when you press a key on your keyboard?
2 How many characters are in the ASCII code?
3 What is the advantage of Unicode over ASCII?
4 Why can Unicode support so many characters (128,000)?

FACT

Nibbles and bytes

You have learned that a computer stores information in bytes. A byte is made up of eight binary digits or bits. You can use more than one byte to store large numbers. You can store very large numbers by using several bytes.

Sometimes you need smaller units of storage. You can use half a byte, which is made up of four binary digits. Computer scientists call half a byte a nibble.

Key words

ASCII code: ASCII code is a method for representing letters, symbols and numbers as binary data. It is limited to 128 different characters.

Unicode: Unicode is a method for representing letters, symbols and numbers as binary data. Unicode can manage more characters than ASCII. Unicode enables users of languages such as Chinese Mandarin to represent the characters as binary data.

Review what you have learned about data and the CPU

Overview

In this chapter, we have looked at binary numbers and how the computer uses them.

You have learned how to:

- explain why computers use binary code
- convert decimal numbers into binary
- convert binary numbers into decimal
- explain how counting works in decimal and binary

- explain how computers use binary numbers to store useful information such as text and symbols
- explain why a computer needs to use code to communicate
- encode and decode simple messages.

 Test questions

Answer these questions to check how well you learned this topic.

1 What is a binary number?

2 How is the decimal 27 represented as a binary number?

3 What is the name of a single binary digit?

4 What is a byte?

5 What is the ASCII code for a character?

6 What do the letters CPU represent?

7 Why is clock speed important in a computer?

8 What does a microprocessor do?

9 In what format do computers transfer data?

10 How is the binary number 01001011 represented in decimal?

 Assessment activities

You can send messages to a partner using a code. You can use the Caesar cipher or Morse code. We have been learning about binary and about ASCII codes. Work with a partner in these activities.

Starter activity

In ASCII code the capital letter A is represented by the decimal number 65. The capital letter Z is represented by the decimal number 90.

1 List the upper-case letters of the alphabet. Write the correct decimal number next to each letter (for example, A   65).

2 Convert each decimal number into binary and write the result as a byte next to the decimal number (for example, A   65   01000001).

3 Use the table you have created to write a short message using the ASCII code.

4 Send the message to your partner. Can your partner work out your message?

Intermediate activity

In this activity you are going to design your own code to send secret messages in binary. Create instructions so that your partner can send a message that only you can decode.

1 Design a code that uses binary numbers to represent the letters of the alphabet. Create a table that lists the alphabet with the binary code for each letter written next to it. There is no need to do anything complicated for this step.

2 Design a substitution code that uses a key.

3 Write clear rules that explain to your partner how to create a coded message. You cannot speak at any time.

4 Your written instructions must include:

- the way you created the binary numbers from the alphabet

- how your substitution code works

- the key your partner should use to send a message.

5 Pass your instructions to your partner.

6 Write a note asking your partner to write a short coded message and send it to you. Can you decode it?

Extension activity

↗ Create a presentation that explains how to convert a decimal number to binary.

↗ Write your instructions as clear simple steps.

↗ Use a software package of your choice. Presentation software may be helpful.

4 Introducing Python

Make a quiz

Overview

In this chapter you will write a computer quiz that will test students. After every question the computer will tell you whether you got the answer right. At the end of the quiz the computer will tell you your score.

Learning outcomes

In Chapter 2, App Inventor, you made a program using App Inventor. In this chapter you will learn to make a program using a different programming language. The new language is called Python. Python is a text-based language which means you make the program using written commands, not blocks.

By the end of this chapter you will know how to:

- ↗ write a program in Python
- ↗ create a program with inputs, outputs and processes
- ↗ plan a program by setting out an algorithm
- ↗ use if... else and a logical test to vary the output of a program
- ↗ use variables and change the value of a variable
- ↗ use relational and arithmetic operators.

Talk about...

Some students like tests that are run by the computer. They don't worry much about getting the answers right. Would you prefer a test marked by your teacher or by a computer? What are the advantages and the disadvantages of each method?

Computers can be used to collect medical details or other information that people might feel is hard to share with a person face to face. What are the advantages and disadvantages of this?

Create a quiz

In this chapter you will create a multiple choice quiz. Your teacher will give you a quiz topic, or let you choose a topic for the quiz.

- Work in groups to develop a set of ten questions for the quiz.
- For each question, note the right answer and three wrong answers.
- Don't make it too obvious what the right answer is.

F|A|C|T

Python

In this chapter you will use a programming language called Python. A python is a type of snake, but the story is that the name Python for the programming language is a reference to something else. There used to be a comedy show called Monty Python's Flying Circus. The creators of the Python programming language were big fans of that show. They used the name Python for their programming language as a tribute to their favourite show.

Program

Assign a value   Prompt   Run

Information   Comment   Machine code

Interpreter   If
          Relational operator   Language
          IDLE
Indented   Instruction
          Else
Calculations   Arithmetic operator

Logical operator

Learning outcomes

In this lesson you will enter some simple Python commands.

When you have completed this lesson you will be able to:

↗ write a program in Python

↗ create a program with inputs, outputs and processes.

⌘ Learn about...

You have learned that the actions of a computer are controlled by software. A software app (or application) is a set of stored instructions. When the computer reads the instructions it carries out the actions. Different apps contain different instructions, so they make the computer do different things.

The instructions are stored inside the computer using a digital code (a number code). The instructions are called **machine code**.

Most programmers do not write software using machine code. Instead they write instructions in a programming language. There are many different programming languages. You have learned to use a programming language called App Inventor. In this chapter you will learn to write programs in a different programming language, called Python.

The program code you write must be turned into machine code that the computer can understand.

What is an interpreter?

An **interpreter** is software that turns a program into machine code. An interpreter converts one line of the program into machine code. Then it carries out the instruction in that line of code. When it has done that it goes on to convert the next line.

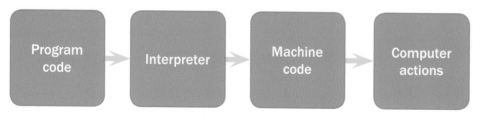

In this chapter you will write code and **run** the code. When you run the code the interpreter will turn it into machine code, and carry out the instructions.

⏻ How to...

You write Python code in a window called the Integrated Development Environment. Python abbreviates this to IDLE. So the first action is to start IDLE. Find the IDLE icon on the Start menu or the Desktop.

When you start IDLE you should see a window called Python Shell.

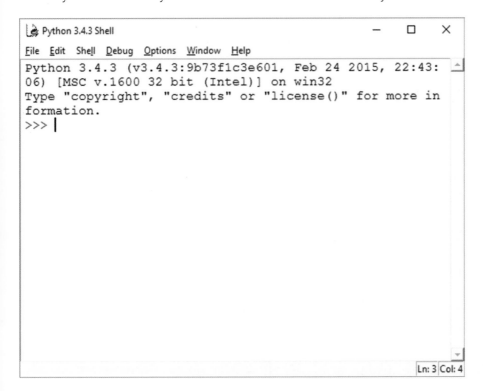

Enter commands

Now you can enter your first Python command. The print command is used to produce output on the screen. A print command looks like this.

```
print("…")
```

You must type print in lower-case letters not upper case (no capitals). All Python command words must be written in lower case. If you forget, Python will not recognise the word.

The command must include the brackets and quote marks as shown here. Instead of the dots between the quote marks you can type any text that you like. For example:

```
print("I am learning Python")
print("My name is Alison")
print("these    words    are    really    far    apart")
```

In computer code, a sequence of letters or other characters is called a string. When you press the Enter key the computer will display the string, just as you entered it.

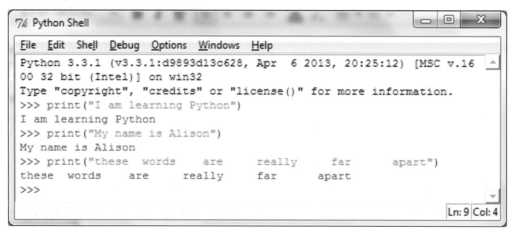

Notice how IDLE uses colour to show the different types of text: the print command in purple, the string in green, and the output in blue.

Print the evidence

When you have entered a series of Python commands you can print the contents of the IDLE window. This will provide evidence of your achievement. Open the File menu and choose Print Window. If this doesn't work take a screen shot, or let your teacher see your code.

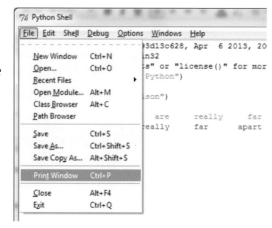

The same menu has the option to Exit from IDLE. Pick that option when you have finished.

Now you do it...

1 Start Python on your computer.

2 Enter several print commands to produce different outputs on the screen.

3 Print out the IDLE window to show your achievement.

 ## If you have time...

You have used the print command to print strings. You can also use the print command to show the result of calculations. Here are some examples:

- ↗ `print(3+6)`
- ↗ `print(99/3)`
- ↗ `print(8*5)`

Notice that you do not use quote marks in calculations.

Experiment with using the print command to do calculations. Make more complex examples using more than two numbers. Print out your results.

Test yourself...

1 Name two different programming languages.

2 What is shown in green in a Python program?

3 Write the Python code that would print out the name of your school.

4 What is the job of a piece of software called an interpreter?

5 Here are two different Python commands. What is the output on the screen following each command?

```
print(100/4)
print("100/4")
```

FACT

Python is free

Python is free software. As well as using Python at school you can put it onto any other computer for no cost. Go to this website:

`www.python.org/downloads/`

If you put Python on your computer at home you can practise programming outside lesson time.

Key words

Interpreter: An interpreter is software that turns a line of program code into machine code.

Machine code: Machine code consists of the digital signals that tell a computer what action to carry out.

Run: Run is when program code is turned into machine code and the instructions are carried out.

Learning outcomes

In Lesson 4.1 you entered Python commands one at a time. In this lesson you will store a series of commands as a program.

When you have completed this lesson you will be able to:

↗ write a program in Python

↗ create a program with inputs, outputs and processes.

⌘ Learn about...

In Lesson 4.1 you typed a single line of Python code. When you pressed the Enter key, the code was sent to the interpreter. The interpreter turned the code into a computer command. Then the computer followed the command and carried out the action.

In this lesson you will store several lines of code as a Python **program**. Then you will run the program. The computer will carry out every command in the program.

Your program will use:

↗ print commands

↗ comment lines.

You learned to use print commands in Lesson 4.1. The special print command:

```
print("\n")
```

makes a blank line.

Comment lines

As well as commands for the computer, a program can include **comments**. The computer ignores the comments. The comments are just for human readers to help someone else understand your code.

In Python every comment begins with this symbol:

#

When the computer sees this symbol it knows it must ignore the rest of the line. In the IDLE window, comments are shown in red text. In this program you can use comment lines to introduce the program.

 # How to...

You have been working in a window with the heading Python Shell. Now open a second window. In this window you will make a Python program. Open the File menu and select New File.

Enter the program

Here is an example program. As you learned in Lesson 4.1, IDLE uses colour to show the different types of code. Red is for comments, purple is for the print function and green is for the strings.

```
74 *QuizMaker in development.py - C:/Python33/QuizMaker in development.py*

File  Edit  Format  Run  Options  Windows  Help
# Program name: QuizMaker
# Written by  : Alison Page
# A multiple choice quiz that gives you the score

print("WELCOME TO THE QUIZ")
print("====================")
print("\n")

#question one

print("1. What gas is needed for respiration?")
print("\n")
print("A: Oxygen")
print("B: Nitrogen")
print("C: Hydrogen")
print("D: Argon")

                                                   Ln: 17 Col: 0
```

Four of the lines are comments. The comment lines make a message for the human reader. The computer ignores these lines. The other lines are print commands. They will produce the output of the program.

Save the program

Open the file menu and click Save As. Save the file using a suitable name. The name must be one word with no spaces. We have called our program QuizMaker.

Run the program

To run the program, open the Run menu and select Run Module.

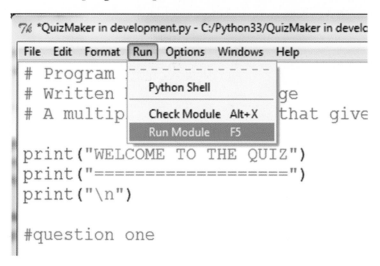

Syntax errors

The rules of a programming language are called syntax. If your code is not exactly right it will make a syntax error. The program will not run. You will see an error message.

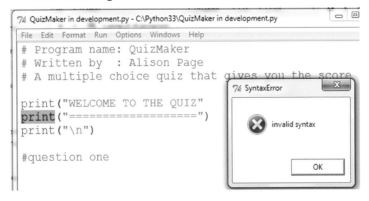

The computer has highlighted where it noticed the error. The error is in the line above the highlight. Can you spot it?

If you see an error message, make the correction and run the program again.

Program output

The output of the program will appear in the other IDLE window (the Python Shell window). The output will look like this.

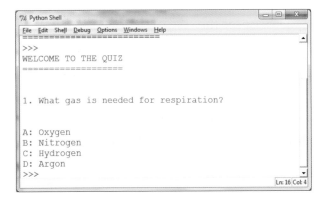

Ahmed completed this activity. He changed the program. The output of his program looks like this.

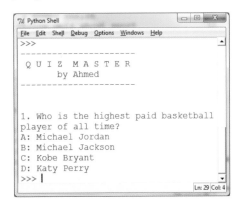

Ahmed changed the heading and the question. Do you know the right answer to his question?

Now you do it...

1 Create a program that displays the title and first question of a quiz. Like Ahmed, design your own output screen. Your output screen doesn't have to look the same as Ahmed's.

2 Save the file using a suitable file name. Run the program.

3 Print out the Program window and the Python Shell window to show your achievement.

 If you have time...

Invent a multiple choice quiz that has ten questions on a topic of your choice. Use Python commands to display the quiz.

This command:

```
input("press ENTER key to continue")
```

will make the program pause. The program will wait for the user to press the Enter key. Add this command after each question so the user has a chance to read it.

 Test yourself...

1 Explain what this Python command does:

```
print("\n")
```

2 You have two windows open on the screen: a Python program file and the Python Shell. When you run a program, where does the output appear?

3 Identify the syntax error in this line of code:

```
Print("What is the right answer?")
```

4 What is the effect of the # symbol in Python code?

Key words

Comment: A comment is a line in a program that the computer will ignore. A comment is used to show messages for the human reader.

Program: A program is a file that stores many lines of code.

Learning outcomes

You have learned to make a Python program that displays output. In this lesson you will learn to use a variable to store input.

When you have completed this lesson you will be able to:

↗ use variables to store values

↗ allow the user to input new values.

⌘ Learn about...

Every computer has memory. Computer memory can store changing data values. Each value is stored in a different area of memory. In programming you can name a memory area. You can use the memory area to store changing data values. In programming, this named storage area is called a variable.

A variable is like a box with a name written on it. This variable is called answer.

You can store anything you like in the box. The data value stored in the box can vary, but the name of the variable stays the same.

Variable name

Every variable needs a name. You can choose any name you like. A good variable name will remind you of what data the variable stores. Two variable names from the quiz program are:

↗ score

↗ answer

What data do you think will be stored in each of these variables?

Data type

Every variable has a data type. Different types of data are stored in different ways in the computer. Python looks at the type of data you have put into the variable and decides what type of storage to use.

In this lesson you will make a program with two variables. The two variables store different types of data.

➤ The variable `score` stores the value 0. Python will use number storage.

➤ The variable `answer` will store a letter typed by the user. Python will use character storage.

 How to...

A variable is like an empty box. You must put data into the variable. You **assign a value** to the variable. You do this with the equals sign.

```
variable = value
```

First, type the name of the variable. Then type the equals sign. Then type the value you want to put in that variable. So, for example, at the start of the quiz your score is 0. Here is the command to assign the value 0 to the variable.

```
score = 0
```

You use this method when you know exactly what value should go into the variable.

Input a value

Another way to put data into a variable is to allow user input. A user is any person who runs your program. User input is anything the user types in. To assign user input to a variable you use an equals sign and the word 'input'.

This command will assign the value that the user types in, to the variable called `answer`:

```
answer = input()
```

You can also add a message to users. The message will tell users what they should type in. This message is called a **prompt**. Here is an example.

```
answer = input("Type a letter A-D: ")
```

You use the input method when you want users to choose the value that goes into the variable.

Example

Here is the quiz program. Two new lines of code have been added. Each line creates a variable and assigns a value. Can you see the lines?

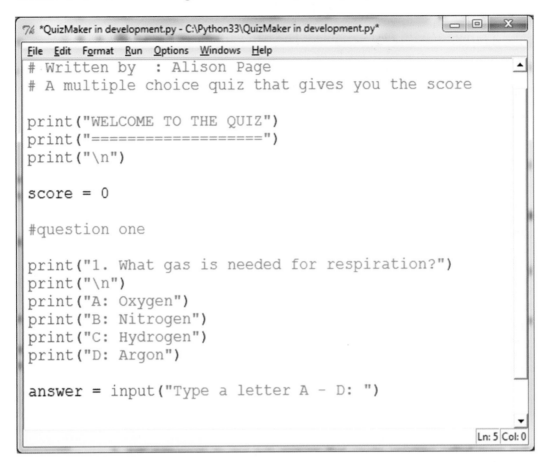

```
# Written by  : Alison Page
# A multiple choice quiz that gives you the score

print("WELCOME TO THE QUIZ")
print("===================")
print("\n")

score = 0

#question one

print("1. What gas is needed for respiration?")
print("\n")
print("A: Oxygen")
print("B: Nitrogen")
print("C: Hydrogen")
print("D: Argon")

answer = input("Type a letter A - D: ")
```

⊕ Now you do it...

1. Add a new line to your quiz program to create a variable called `score`. Assign the value `0` to `score`.

2. Add a new line to your quiz program to create a variable called `answer`. This variable will hold user input.

3. Save and run the program. Print the program and the output to show your achievement.

🌐 If you have time...

This command will add 1 to the score:

```
score = score + 1
```

This command will print the score:

```
print(score)
```

Add commands to your program so the score goes up by 1 after every question. At the end of the quiz the computer will show the score.

 **Test yourself...**

1 Every variable must have a name. Explain how to choose a good name for a variable.

2 Here is a line of Python. What is the name of the variable? What value is assigned to the variable?

```
age = 15
```

3 Write a line of code that lets the user input a value to the variable `name`. Make sure you include a prompt to tell the user what to enter.

4 Write a line of code that prints out the value stored in the variable `name`.

Key words

Assign a value: When you assign a value to a variable you put some data into the variable. The data will be stored in the variable.

Prompt: A prompt is a message to the user. The prompt tells the user what value to enter into a variable.

4.4 Plan a process

Learning outcomes

You have learned to make a Python program. The program has inputs and outputs. In this lesson you will learn how to plan a program, so that it produces the outputs your client wants.

When you have completed this lesson you will be able to:

↗ plan a program by setting out an algorithm

↗ use a logical test to vary the output of a program.

⌘ Learn about...

A process is a set of actions that produce a result. In Chapter 1, Computational thinking, you learned that a process can be used to solve a problem. A process causes changes. There are processes in the natural world. For example, a fire changes fuel into heat and light. Photosynthesis changes carbon dioxide into oxygen.

Photosynthesis is a natural process

Computers can help us with processing tasks. This lesson is about computer processes.

A computer process changes data into information. Data are facts and figures. The output of a computer process is **information**. Information is data that have been organised or changed to make them more useful.

In Chapter 2, App Inventor, you learned that programmers work for a client or customer. The program has to meet the client's requirements. The program turns input into output to meet those requirements. If the program produces the right output, then the client will value it.

A computer process turns data into information

An algorithm describes a process

In Chapter 1, Computational thinking, you learned about algorithms. An algorithm sets out the steps that produce the result you want. You described algorithms using a flow chart.

Programmers have to plan the processes used in a program before they begin to write the program code. A programmer may use a flow chart to plan a program.

Planning the algorithm before starting work helps the programmer. The algorithm:

↗ guides the programmer's work as he or she writes the program
↗ helps explain the program to other people—for example, the programmer may wish to share the program with other members of the team.
↗ keeps a record of what the program does
↗ helps to reduce errors.

Avoiding errors

In Lesson 4.2 you learned about syntax errors. If there are syntax errors in a Python program, it will not run. The computer will show an error message. That makes it easy to spot syntax errors.

There are other types of error. For example, if the user answers a question wrongly but the computer says, 'The answer is right' then that is an error. The error is not a syntax error as it does not break the rules of the Python language. The computer will not show an error message because it is not a syntax error.

This type of error is called a logical error because it makes the computer do something illogical. Logical errors can be hard to spot. For this reason a programmer must:

↗ plan a program carefully to avoid logical errors
↗ test a program thoroughly to find any errors.

⏻ How to...

A programmer plans a program by thinking about input, output and processing. Here is an outline plan for the QuizMaker program.

↗ Output: the computer shows a question.
↗ Input: the user enters an answer.
↗ Process: the computer checks the answer to see whether it is right.
↗ Output: a message says whether the answer is right or wrong.

Logical tests and decisions

In Chapter 2, App Inventor, you learned about logical tests. A logical test has the result 'true' ('yes') or 'false' ('no'). You can use the equals sign to make a logical test. The QuizMaker program uses this type of logical test.

↗ Does the given answer = the right answer?

Before you go any further, think about what you want the program to do. Answer these questions.

* What is the output if the answer is right?
* What is the output if the answer is wrong?

Using an algorithm to show a process

In Chapter 1, Computational thinking, you learned how to use a flow chart to show an algorithm. Programmers can use a flow chart algorithm to plan a program. Here is part of a flow chart used to plan the QuizMaker program.

To complete the flow chart you must decide what actions the computer will take.

* What is the output if the result of the logical test is 'true'?
* What is the output if the result of the logical test is 'false'?

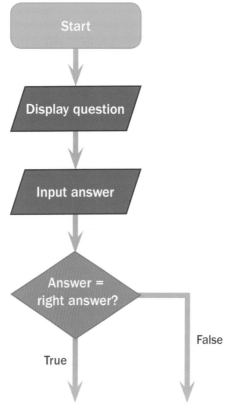

⊕ Now you do it...

1 Decide the actions that the computer will take after the logical test. There will be different actions depending on whether the result of the test is 'true' or 'false'.

2 Draw a flow chart to show the complete algorithm. Remember that an algorithm finishes in a single 'Stop' box.

If you have time...

↗ Use a suitable graphics package to make a high-quality version of the flow chart.

Test yourself...

1 Why is it easier to spot a syntax error than a logical error?
2 What flow chart shape is used to show a logical test?
3 Explain the benefits a programmer gets from setting out the algorithm of a program before starting work.
4 In Chapter 2, App Inventor, you made an app that showed an ID card. What were the inputs, processes and outputs of that app?

Key words

Information: Information is data that have been processed to make them more organised or more useful.

Your answer: right or wrong

Learning outcomes

You have planned a quiz program. Your plan uses a logical test. In this lesson you will use the `if... else` structure to turn the plan into a working program.

When you have completed this lesson you will be able to:

↗ use relational operators

↗ use `if... else` and a logical test to vary the output of a program.

⌘ Learn about...

In Lesson 4.4 you planned a program. You made a flow chart to show the algorithm of the program. The flow chart included a logical test. The test was: Did the user enter the right answer? This flow chart shows the completed algorithm.

The algorithm has two possible routes. The computer will take one of the routes. The computer chooses a route based on the result of the logical test.

A structure with two routes and a logical test is called a conditional structure.

Relational operators

A logical test can compare two values. To make the comparison you use a **relational operator**.

In Chapter 2, App Inventor, you used a simple equals sign as a relational operator.

Here are four of the most important relational operators used in Python.

Relational operator	What it means
==	The two values are the same
!=	The two values are different
<	The first value is smaller
>	The first value is bigger

Comparing values

To make a logical test you can use a relational operator to compare two values. Then the computer checks the comparison to see whether it is true. Here are some examples.

Start → Output question → Input answer → Answer = right answer? → True: Output "You are right" / False: Output "You are wrong" → Stop

Logical test	Is the result 'true' or 'false'?
(3 + 2) == 5	TRUE
(7 + 8) == 21	FALSE
8 > 5	TRUE
99 > 109	FALSE
(100 + 1) ! = 101	FALSE

Copy the table. Add three new rows with extra examples of logical tests.

 # How to...

In most programming languages you make a conditional structure using the word '**if**'.

1 You start with the word 'if'.

2 Next you enter a logical test.

3 After the logical test you enter a block of code.

The block of code is only carried out `if` the result of the test is 'true'. Here is an example.

```
#question one

print("What gas is needed for respiration?")
print("\n")
print("A: Oxygen")
print("B: Nitrogen")
print("C: Hydrogen")
print("D: Argon")

answer = input("Enter a letter A-D: ")
print("\n")

if answer == "A":
    print("You got it right")
```

The last two lines in this program are a conditional structure using the word 'if'.

↗ The conditional structure starts with the word `if`

↗ Next comes a logical test. In this case the test is `answer == "A"`

↗ After the logical test comes a colon **:**

The block of code that follows the `if` statement is **indented**. That means there is white space between the left margin and the line. The lines which are indented will only be carried out if the result of the test is 'true'. They will only be carried out if the user enters an upper-case letter 'A' Any other letter, even a lower-case 'a', will not work.

How to use `if... else` in a Python program

You can now add a second block of code. The second block of code will be carried out if the result of the logical test is 'false'. The block is called an **else**

```python
if answer == "A":
    print("You got it right")
else:
    print("You got it wrong")
```

statement.

When you type this, IDLE will add the colour and the indentation automatically.

Improve the output

If you have time you can improve the program output. You can change the

```python
if answer == "A":
    print("Yes, oxygen is needed for respiration. You win!")
else:
    print("No, the answer is A (oxygen). Better luck next time")
```

message to the user. Here is an example.

Many questions

You can add more questions to your program. Just enter a new question, using the same method as before. Make sure the lines of the new question are not indented. They are not part of the conditional structure.

This image shows part of a program. A second question has been added about the capital of Japan. The second question follows on from the question about oxygen. Questions can be on any subject you choose.

```python
if answer == "A":
    print("Yes, oxygen is needed for respiration. You win!")
else:
    print("No, the answer is A (oxygen). Better luck next time")

#question two

print("\n")
print("What is the capital of Japan?")
print("\n")
print("A: Beijing")
print("B: Kyoto")
print("C: Tokyo")
print("D: Honshu")

answer = input("Enter a letter A-D: ")
print("\n")

if answer == "C":
    print("Yes, Tokyo has been the capital since 1868. You win!")
```

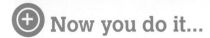 Now you do it...

1 Your program should have at least one question in it. Add a conditional structure after the question. This will tell users whether they got the answer right.

2 Add at least one more question to your program.

3 Save and run the program.

4 Print the program and the output to show your achievement.

 If you have time...

Expand your quiz program so that it has ten questions. Add a conditional structure after each question.

 Test yourself...

Look at this code then answer the questions.

```
elevenplus = input("Are you age 11 or over? (Y/N): ")

if elevenplus == "Y":
    print("You can ride the roller coaster")
else:
    print("Not old enough for this ride")
```

1 A variable is used in this code. What is the name of the variable?

2 What relational operator is used in this code?

3 What logical test is used in this program? What is the meaning of this logical test?

4 What is the output if the result of this logical test is 'false'?

Key words

Else: In programming the word `else` comes before code which is only carried out if the result of the test is 'false'.

If: The word `if` introduces a conditional structure in a computer program. `if` is followed by a logical test and a block of code. The block of code is only carried out if the result of the test is 'true'.

Indented: Lines that are set in from the left margin.

Relational operator: A relational operator is a symbol that compares two values.

Learning outcomes

You have made a quiz program with two or more questions. The computer checks the answer to each question. The computer says whether users got the answer right or wrong. Now you will complete the program by adding a scoring system. The score will increase by 1 every time users give a correct answer. At the end of the quiz users will see their score.

When you have completed this lesson you will be able to:

↗ use variables and change the value of a variable

↗ use relational and arithmetic operators.

⌘ Learn about...

In Lesson 4.3 you learned how to create a new variable. You gave the variable a name, and assigned a value. For example, one variable was called `score`. You set the value of this variable to `0`.

```
score = 0
```

You can also set the value of a variable using a calculation.

Arithmetic operators

To make a calculation you use an **arithmetic operator**, such as 'add' or 'multiply'. Here are four of the most important arithmetic operators used in Python.

Arithmetic operator	What it does
+	Add together
–	Take away
*	Multiply
/	Divide

Increase a variable by 1

If the user gets an answer right, the score goes up by 1. The Python command to increase the value of a variable by 1 is:

```
score = score + 1
```

This command tells the computer to change the value of the variable `score`. The command will increase the value by 1. This type of calculation is very common in programming.

⏻ How to...

At the start of the program the score is set to 0. The user has not answered any questions yet.

If the user gets an answer right, the score goes up by 1. You must put the command inside the conditional structure. The line is indented. The command will only be carried out if the result of the logical test is 'true'.

```
score = 0

#question one

print("What gas is needed for respiration?")
print("\n")
print("A: Oxygen")
print("B: Nitrogen")
print("C: Hydrogen")
print("D: Argon")

answer = input("Enter a letter A-D: ")
print("\n")

if answer == "A":
    print("Yes, oxygen is needed for respiration. You win!")
    score = score + 1
else:
    print("No, the answer is A (oxygen). Better luck next time")
```

Make sure you add this code to every question in the quiz.

Output the score

At the end of the quiz you add code to print out the score. You should also add some words to explain what the score is.

You can do it using two print commands like this:

```
print("Quiz completed. Your score was ")

print(score)
```

Or you can combine the text and the variable into one print command. There is a comma in between the two.

```
print("Your final score was: ", score)
```

⊕ Now you do it...

1   Add code to every question in your quiz to increase the score by 1 if the user gets the answer right.

2   Add code at the end of the quiz that displays the final score.

3   Save, run and print to show your achievement.

What are logical operators?

At the moment the logical test for each question looks like this.

```
if answer == "A":
```

Users only pass this test if they enter an upper-case letter 'A'. If they enter a lower-case letter 'a' that counts as a wrong answer.

You can help users by making a change to the program. You can change the program so that it will accept either 'A' or 'a' as the right answer. You can make this change using a **logical operator**. A logical operator lets you join several tests together to make one big test.

Logical operator	Example	What it means
and	X and Y	Both results are 'true'
or	X or Y	At least one result is 'true'
not	Not X	A result is 'false'

You can change the program so that users pass the test if they type 'A' or 'a'.

Here is the program showing this change.

Logical operators can also be called Boolean operators.

```
if answer == "A" or answer == "a":
    print("Yes, oxygen is needed for respiration. You win!")
    score = score + 1
else:
    print("No, the answer is A (oxygen). Better luck next time")
```

🌐 If you have time...

↗   Use the logical operator `or` to improve the logical test in all your quiz questions.

↗   Make sure your quiz includes ten questions.

↗   Save and print the program to show your achievement.

Test yourself...

1   What arithmetic operator is used to multiply two numbers?

2   Write a line of code that outputs the value of a variable called `age`.

3   Extend the code you wrote for question 2 so that the program also outputs some text explaining what the variable is.

4   A programmer decided that if the user answered a really difficult question correctly, the score would go up by 2. Write the line of code that increases the variable `score` by 2.

5   You want to check that two logical tests are BOTH true. What logical operator would you use?

FACT

George Boole (1815–1864)

Boolean operators are named after an English mathematician called George Boole. He developed many of the logical methods we use in modern programming.

Key words

Arithmetic operator: An arithmetic operator is a symbol that carries out a calculation.

Logical operator: A logical operator is a term that lets you join several logical tests together. It is also called a Boolean operator.

Review what you have learned about Python

Overview

In this chapter you have learned how to:

↗ write a program in Python

↗ create a program with inputs, outputs and processes

↗ plan a program by setting out an algorithm

↗ use `if... else` and a logical test to vary the output of a program

↗ use variables and change the value of a variable

↗ use relational and arithmetic operators.

 Test questions

Answer these questions to check how well you have learned this topic.

1 What happens when you assign a value to a variable?

2 Write a line of code that assigns the value 50 to a variable called `cost`.

3 Write a line of code that increases the value of the variable `cost` by 5.

4 List four relational operators and explain their meaning.

5 How do you indicate a comment in Python? What are comments used for?

6 What is the difference between data and information?

7 What does software called an interpreter do?

8 Why does a programmer plan an algorithm before beginning to write a program?

9 Write a logical test that gives the result 'true' if a variable age is greater than 18.

10 Here is an extract from a Python program:

```python
if score > 75:

    print("you have passed the test")
```

Extend this code to show a message if the score is not more than 75.

 Assessment activities

A programmer writes a Python program to check a password. Here is the program.

```python
password = input("Enter the password - ")

if password == "Enterprise":
    print("Password is correct")
```

Complete these activities. As you finish each activity, print the code listing and the output screen to show your achievement.

Starter activity

Start Python and enter this program code. Look out for syntax errors, and correct any mistakes you make. Run the program.

Describe in your own words what the program does.

Intermediate activity

Extend the program so that the computer displays a message to users who get the password wrong.

Extension activity

The password program was used to let users log on to a computer game site. There was a problem. Many users forgot to put an upper-case letter at the start of the password. (They typed 'enterprise' instead of 'Enterprise'.)

1   Fix the program so that users can log on successfully if they type either 'Enterprise' or 'enterprise'.

2   Run tests on the program and record your test results.

Information Technology

Computer hardware and software

Overview

Computers are useful for work and for fun, but you also need to know how to use computers safely. In this chapter you will learn about common hardware and how it is used. You will also look at the differences between system and application software. You have probably used most of the software and hardware you will meet in this chapter. However, you may not know all the things hardware and software can do. You also may not know how software and hardware interact with each other.

You need to use computers safely and securely. In this chapter you will learn how to protect yourself online and how to use the Internet responsibly.

Learning outcomes

By the end of this chapter you will know how to:

↗ explain the difference between a manual and an automatic input device

↗ describe a variety of external input, output and storage devices

↗ explain and give examples of system and application software

↗ explain the relationship between user, software and hardware

↗ describe different types of computer network and explain their advantages and disadvantages

↗ describe e-safety

↗ understand where to get help if you need it

↗ stay safe online.

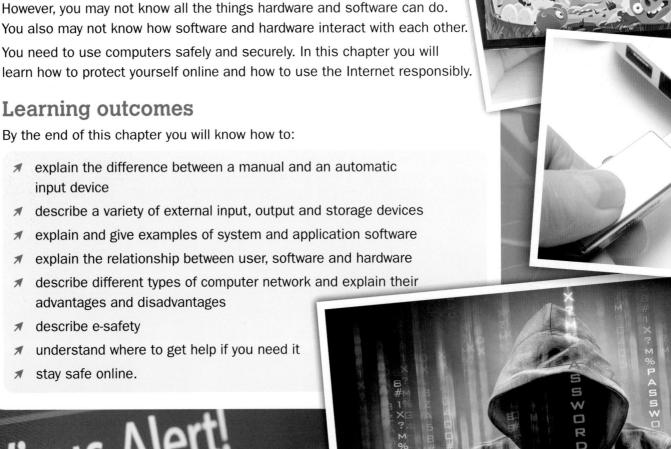

Using your device

- What electronic devices do you use? What devices do your friends use? When and where do you use your devices?

- In pairs, write a list of the electronic devices you use and compare your list with your partner's list. Do you use the same devices in different places and at different times? What do you like about using these devices and why?

- Have you always used the same devices? For example, two years ago did you use the same device that you use now? What do you predict for two years in the future?

- Apps are pieces of software on a phone and tablet. Which are your favourite apps?

F|A|C|T

The first hard disk drive

The first hard disk drive was created by IBM in San Jose, California, USA in 1956. The disk drive was part of the IBM 305 RAMAC, which stands for Random Access Method of Accounting and Control. The disk drive stored only 5 megabytes of data and was as large as a cupboard. It would take about 100,000 of these disk drives to equal the storage of one laptop today.

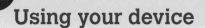

Input device

Storage device

Output device   Automatic input device

Operating system

Manual input device

Application software   Social network

System software

Phishing   Malware   e-safety

LAN

Firewall

WAN

Learning outcomes

When you have completed this lesson you will be able to:

↗ explain the difference between a manual and an automatic input device

↗ describe a variety of external input devices.

 Learn about...

Hardware is any physical part of a computer system. Hardware can be internal (inside the computer) or external (outside the computer).

Some types of hardware are input, output and storage devices. Some devices can act as both an input and an output device. This lesson will focus on input devices.

Input devices

You will remember from Chapter 2, App Inventor, that an input is data that a computer receives. An **input device** is a piece of hardware that you can use to enter data into a computer system. You use an input device to tell a computer what data you want it to process. An input device converts real-world data into a form a computer can understand.

There are two types of input device: manual and automatic.

Manual input devices

Manual input devices are used to input data by hand. The most common of these are a keyboard, mouse or touchscreen.

Keyboard

A keyboard is divided into sections. Other than the standard letter and number keys, there are also direction keys that control the cursor and function keys. Function keys perform special tasks. For example, if you press F7 while using Microsoft Word, you will start the spell check.

Point or point-and-click devices

A mouse is a point-and-click device that is best used on a flat surface. You will already know how a mouse works, but there are other pointing devices that you may find useful. A trackball works in the same way as a mouse but uses a ball that you can roll to control the cursor. Trackballs can be helpful to people who have restricted mobility in their hands. Trackballs are also often used with computer-aided design (CAD) software. Architects, artists, engineers and designers use CAD software to create complicated drawings and illustrations.

Other examples of manual input devices include a touchscreen, webcam, microphone, video game controller and digital camera.

Touchscreen	Webcam	Microphone	Video game controller	Digital camera
You can input information by touching pictures or words on the **touchscreen**. You may have come across touchscreens on smart phones, iPads or other tablets.	A **webcam** can input data by capturing your photo or video on the computer.	You can use a **microphone** to input sound. A microphone used with voice recognition software and a word processor will help the computer write what you say. Voice recognition software helps a computer understand human speech.	You use a **video game controller** to tell your computer what you want your game to do.	A **digital camera** can take photos or video and stores data on a memory card. You can transfer data directly from the memory card or over a USB connection.

Think about the different input devices you have used today. You may have used a smart phone. Smart phones have a touchscreens camera and microphone. You can capture a video of a friend by using the camera. You use your finger on the touchscreen to open the camera app. The camera will let you preview the picture of your friend. The microphone will capture the sound. You are using a combination of input devices.

Automatic input devices

Automatic input devices read and input data into a computer system. Automatic input devices are quicker and usually make fewer mistakes than manual input devices. Examples of automatic input devices include barcode readers, scanners and sensors.

An important difference between manual and automatic input devices is that automatic input devices are designed to do a particular job. For example, the scanner you see built into a supermarket checkout is good at reading information from barcodes. The scanner reads the barcode information quickly and accurately. However, the scanner could not be used for writing an email. Manual input devices are much more flexible. They can be used for all sorts of jobs.

Barcode reader

A **barcode reader** is a device that scans a barcode by shining a light onto it. You can see a barcode reader when you go to the supermarket, department store or library. Barcode readers are mainly used at the cash till to automatically read the price of an item.

Scanner

A **scanner** is a device that reads information or images into a computer. Scanners allow you to take a printed picture or document so that your computer can read and display it. For example, you can scan your fingerprint to gain access to a room. You can also scan a page from your favourite book or a drawing that you created. You can then edit or display these on your computer.

Some scanners are **biometric**. Biometric means that scanners can use data which record some feature of your body, such as a fingerprint or even your voice, as input.

Sensor

A **sensor** is a device that is looking for some type of input from the physical environment. This could be light, heat, motion, moisture, pressure or any one of many other environmental inputs. Weather stations use sensors to automatically tell the computer live weather conditions such as the temperature and wind speed.

Alarm systems use motion and pressure sensors to detect intruders. Fire alarms use heat and smoke detectors to protect us against fire in the home and at school.

Now you do it...

1 Search online to find an image of your favourite games console.

2 How does the games console input information? For example, does the device use touch or sound?

3 On a piece of paper or using drawing software, design a new controller for a games console. How is your design an improvement on the current one?

If you have time...

Research everyday examples of how automatic input devices work.

Supermarkets use barcode readers. The people in the supermarket scan the barcodes on the products. The barcode reader inputs data into the computer system. You can search on the web for more information. Use a search such as:

ICT in supermarkets

↗ What equipment is used in a modern supermarket checkout? Can you find a simple diagram of this equipment?

↗ What is an advantage of using a barcode reader instead of writing the data into a book?

↗ Could there be an error when using a barcode reader? How could an error happen?

↗ Other than in supermarkets, where do you see barcodes in everyday life?

Test yourself...

1 Give an example of an automatic input device. Where would it be used?

2 Give an example of a manual input device. Explain what it does.

3 Is an automatic input device better than a manual input device? Explain your thinking.

4 How could different input sensors improve your life in the future?

Key words

Automatic input device: An automatic input device reads and inputs data into a computer system.

Input device: An input device is a piece of hardware that is used to enter data into a computer system.

Manual input device: A manual input device is used to input data by hand. The most common manual input device is a keyboard or mouse.

How to...

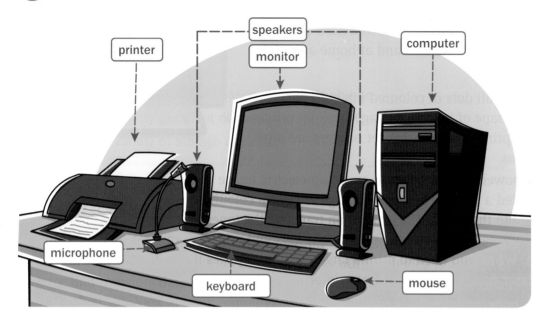

You can learn to identify and describe different types of hardware. Look at the computers in your school. Do they look like the computer in the picture above?

↗   An input device puts data into the computer. Pick up a computer mouse. When you move the mouse, can you see the cursor moving on the screen? The computer mouse is inputting data into the computer.

↗   Look at the keyboard. Using a word-processing program, press the keys on the keyboard. The keyboard is inputting data into the computer.

↗   If your computer has a CD/DVD drive on it, insert a CD or DVD. If the computer can read the CD or DVD, then data will be inputted into the computer.

↗   Look at the computer screen. The computer is putting data onto the screen for you to read. The screen is an output device. It lets you see data coming out of the computer.

↗   If you have a printer attached, you can print the letters and symbols you typed with the keyboard. Data will come out of the computer. The printer is an output device.

↗   If you have a microphone and speakers on your computer, try recording your voice and listening to the recording. Some software tools, such as Google Search or Google Docs, let you dictate your sentences. The microphone is inputting data into the computer. The speakers are outputting data from the computer.

⊕ Now you do it...

Look at this list of devices. Can you find similar examples in your school?

1 Ink-jet printer

2 Computer monitor

3 Set of speakers

4 Microphone

5 Memory stick

Take a photo or sketch a picture of each example you find. Explain whether your example is an input or output device. How did you decide?

🌐 If you have time...

  Imagine you could design a room and have any piece of technology to go into it. For example, you might wish to have large TVs, games consoles and music speakers.

  What would you put into your room? How would you arrange it and why?

  On a piece of paper or using drawing software, draw your room and label the technology. Which items are input devices and which ones are output devices?

  What kind of storage devices will your design use?

📝 Test yourself...

1 Name and describe three output devices.

2 What are the advantages of SSDs?

3 What is the difference between an ink-jet printer and a laser printer?

4 Name a piece of hardware that might be used as both an input and output device.

Key words

Output device: An output device is a piece of hardware that is used to transfer data out of a computer system.

Storage device: A storage device is any piece of computer hardware that is used to record and store data.

Understanding software

Learning outcomes

When you have completed this lesson you will be able to:

↗ explain and give examples of system software

↗ explain and give examples of application software (apps)

↗ explain the relationship between user, software and hardware.

Learn about...

A software program is a set of instructions that directs a computer to carry out tasks. Software makes hardware useful. Software gives hardware the instructions it needs to run. When hardware runs software, it loads the program into its memory.

Software can be divided into two main groups. These are:

↗ **system software**

↗ **application software** (apps).

System software

System software includes operating systems, utility and driver software. The operating system makes all the different parts of the computer work together. Utility software does simple maintenance on the computer. For example, utility software fixes errors on a hard disk. Driver software translates computer instructions so the instructions can be understood by particular input and output devices. For example, the computer can control the camera to take a photo. The computer 'drives' the camera using the driver software.

The **operating system** allows you to use the computer without knowing how to speak the computer's language. Without an operating system, a computer is useless. Operating system software manages all of the computer's hardware and software.

Operating system

The operating system does a number of jobs. These are two of the most important jobs it does.

1 It allows the application software, such as a word processor, to communicate with the computer's hardware. For example, the operating system controls saving files to a storage device and outputting text and images to your screen.

2 It provides a user interface. The user interface is what you use to communicate with the operating system. When you click on a screen to start a game or a word processor, you are using the user interface.

Examples of popular desktop operating systems include Microsoft Windows, Linux and macOS on Apple computers.

Types of operating system

↗ **Microsoft Windows** (referred to simply as Windows) is a graphics-based operating system. Having a graphics-based operating system means you give instructions to Windows by clicking on images on the screen. These images are called icons. Windows uses a graphical user interface or GUI (sometimes pronounced 'gooey') for short. You can use Windows on desktop computers, laptops, tablets and phones. Windows is used on computers that are made by many different companies.

↗ **Linux** is an open-source operating system. Being open source means that the Linux computer code is available for free and can be changed by anyone. Companies including Google and Facebook use the Linux operating system on their computers to make their websites available on the Internet.

↗ **macOS** is an operating system used on Apple computers. macOS is the only operating system for the Apple Mac computers. macOS uses a graphics-based system of icons. Siri, a voice-command tool, is included in macOS. The user can speak words and Siri can search for information or give instructions to the computer.

Mobile operating systems

Examples of popular mobile operating systems include iOS and Android.

↗ **iOS** stands for iPhone operating system. iOS is a mobile operating system created and developed by Apple. iOS is mainly used on Apple's mobile devices, including the iPhone, iPad and iPod touch. For the Apple Watch, the operating system is called iWatch.

↗ **Android** is a mobile operating system designed by Google. Android is used mainly for touch-screen mobile devices, such as smart phones and tablets.

Application software

Apps do the real work when you use a computer. In Chapter 2, App Inventor, you created your own app. You use apps to do many tasks on a computer. For example, you use apps when you write an email, message a friend, listen to music or play a game. Apps include word processors, web browsers and social media software such as Facebook, Twitter and Instagram.

Apps need the operating system software so that they can use the computer's hardware. The operating system lets you use your keyboard and mouse, see your work on screen and save it to disk.

 **How to...**

You can learn to identify the different types of software running on your device. To identify the operating system, shut down the device and start it again. When most devices start up, they will display a message describing the operating system.

When you run a game such as the Angry Birds app on an iPad, the app tells the computer to clear the screen, display a picture and play some music. The app tells the computer how to let you control the game characters when you use input devices, such as the touchscreen or keyboard. The app tells the computer how to handle your input instructions.

Once opened, your app will run using the operating system until you close the app.

In the Angry Birds example, you are the user and the app is the Angry Birds game. The operating system is iOS and the hardware is the iPad.

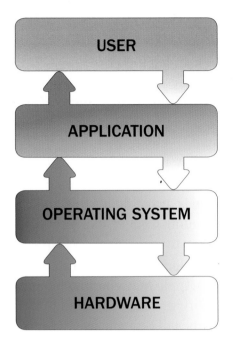

Relationship diagram: the relationship between the user, software and hardware

⊕ Now you do it...

1 Work with a partner to think of another example that shows the relationship between the user, software and hardware. Use the Angry Birds example to help. Think of a creative way to explain your idea using software of your choice. Share your example with the rest of your class.

2 Redraw this image using examples of your own. Use a different example from the one you used in part 1 of this task.

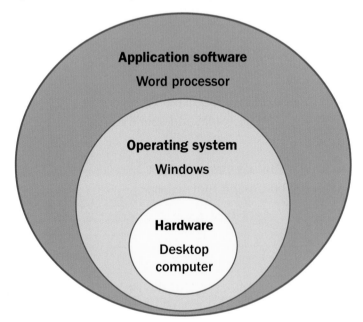

🌐 If you have time...

Think of an operating system you have used. List your favourite features. What would you like to improve?

Test yourself...

1 What is system software? Give two examples.
2 What is an app? Give two examples.
3 Give an example of an operating system that uses a GUI.
4 What is a software program?

Key words

System software: System software manages the computer's hardware and software resources. System software includes operating systems, utility and driver software.

Operating system: The operating system allows the application software (app) to communicate with the computer's hardware.

Application software (app): An app is a program designed to do a specific task.

Connecting computers together

Learning outcomes

When you have completed this lesson you will be able to:

⤢ define different types of computer network

⤢ explain the advantages and disadvantages of different types of network.

⌘ Learn about...

A computer network is where two or more computers are connected together to share data. The two main types of computer network are:

⤢ local area networks (**LANs**)

⤢ wide area networks (**WANs**).

LANs

The computers in your school are likely to be connected to a LAN. Having a LAN means that each computer is connected by cables to a large, powerful computer called a server.

A server provides file storage space and access, for example, to software, the Internet and printers. The server has a large group of disk drives so that you can save your work safely. A server provides security, protecting you from computer virus attacks. You have to log on to the server in order to use the network. You will probably have been given a login name and password for your school.

WANs

A WAN is spread over a large area. WANs are made by joining many local area networks together. The Internet is a WAN.

Advantages of networks

A network can:

⤢ share files easily between computers

⤢ store data on a file server and back it up regularly

⤢ let computers share printers instead of having one each.

⤢ keep all computers on the network up to date.

Disadvantages of networks

There are disadvantages of having a computer network.

⤢ A network can increase costs because it needs cables, servers, switches and hubs.

⤢ A human manager may be needed to maintain the network, making sure it works efficiently, which adds to costs.

- A network may make it easier for a virus to spread, since a network connects computers together.
- A network can lose more data than an individual computer if it is hacked or broken.

How to...

You can learn to identify different types of LAN. Three common types of LAN are: bus, ring and star networks.

- In a bus network, there is one main cable and the computers are connected to that main cable.
- In a ring network, the computers are connected to each other to form a circuit or ring.
- In a star network, the computers are connected to a central hub or switch, which sends and receives the data for each computer.

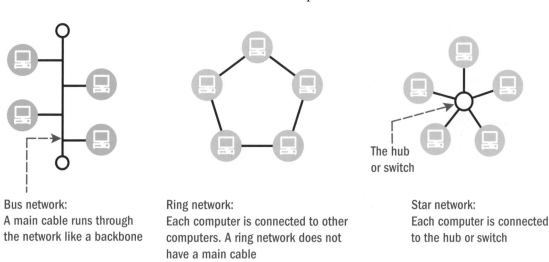

Bus network:
A main cable runs through the network like a backbone

Ring network:
Each computer is connected to other computers. A ring network does not have a main cable

Star network:
Each computer is connected to the hub or switch

The hub or switch

A bus or ring network could be a cheaper option than a star network to connect computers. However, if there is a problem with the cable connections in the bus or ring networks, then the computers may not be able to communicate. A star network has a hub or switch that can continue to send and receive data even if one of the computers has a fault.

Networks in the home

In your home you may have a wireless network, which is often called Wifi. You can connect your laptop computers, tablets and phones to a Wifi system. You use a wireless router or hub to connect to a cable network, either by cables or sometimes by telephone lines. Your Wifi network is a star network, where each device connects to the central hub. Other devices, such as central heating thermostats, lighting controls, security webcams and sensors can also connect to the network. This lets the devices be controlled by the home owners when they are not in the house, for example they can switch on lights or watch the security webcam.

Now you do it...

Go on a wires hunt! You can investigate your school to see if it has a network. Explore how the network is arranged.

1   Start with a room with a computer in it. Is there a network cable attached to the computer? Is the cable plugged into a socket on the wall? Now try another room. Is there a computer connected by a cable?

2   In your school, you may have a wireless network as well as a wired network. Are there any desktop computers or laptops that do not have cables? Can these computers still connect to the network?

3   Does your school have a room with many computers in it? How do these computers connect to the network?

4   Is there a printer that is shared by all the computers in your classroom? Where is that printer?

5   Do you have tablets at your school? Where can the tablets be used? How do the tablets connect to the network?

If you have time...

Mobile phones connect to the mobile phone company's network.

↗   How does the mobile phone connect?

↗   Is there a phone mast near where you live?

 **Test yourself...**

1 Define a computer network.
2 Describe three types of LAN.
3 How is a LAN different from a WAN?
4 Name one advantage and one disadvantage of a star network compared to a ring network.

Key words

LAN: A local area network (LAN) is a network of computers, usually all in the same building.

WAN: A wide area network (WAN) is a network of computers, which are spread over a large distance. The Internet is a WAN.

Learning outcomes

When you have completed this lesson you will be able to:

↗ describe e-safety

↗ understand where to get help if you need it.

⌘ Learn about...

The Internet is a powerful tool for research, news, gaming, entertainment, socialising, communicating and having fun. In order to get the best out of the Internet you should always be prepared and know how to stay safe online.

Communicating online

There are lots of ways to communicate with friends and family online. You may have already used some of these:

↗ chat rooms

↗ instant messaging

↗ **social networks**

↗ email.

Chat rooms

A chat room is a website where people get together online to chat. When people use a chat room they type messages to each other, rather than talk. Sometimes there is a particular subject to a chat room and sometimes people just socialise. Chat rooms work in real time. This means that the people online are all chatting at the same time.

A forum is similar to a chat room, but a forum is usually set up for people to talk about a particular subject. The people in the forum might talk about a popular game or a TV series. People are not always online together. You can post a question or comment and other members of the group will answer you later when they are online.

Chat rooms can be great places for meeting online with friends and for sharing information about your interests. Remember that you need to stay safe online. Do not use your real name in a chat room. You can never be totally sure who you are talking to. Sometimes people may pretend to be someone else. A stranger in a chat room might pretend to be friendly to gain the trust of others and deceive them.

Find out more at the Kidsmart website:

`www.kidsmart.org.uk/chat/`

Instant messaging

Instant messaging allows a person to send a message directly to another person or group of people. The people receiving the message can view it and respond immediately. Instant messaging is similar to a phone conversation, but uses text.

Social networks

A social network is a website or other technology that lets people communicate over the Internet. People communicate informally with others who have similar interests to their own. Facebook, Instagram and Twitter are some of the most common social networking sites. You need to be at least 13 years old to use sites like Facebook and Twitter. You can create your own space on these sites and share your thoughts by posting blogs, photos and even sharing video. Remember that you should only invite or accept invitations from people you know.

Email

Sending email is a fun and easy way to keep in touch with friends and family. Using email, you can send messages, videos or photos. Using an official school or family email account can help keep you safe online. You should only open emails from people you know. You should not open an attachment unless you are expecting one, because an attachment can contain a virus.

 **How to...**

Using the Internet can be great fun. You can learn a lot from people sharing ideas and advice. However, sometimes people may not be kind and helpful, just like some people you might meet face to face.

You can learn to stay safe on the Internet. Follow these rules to stay safe.

1 Always tell an adult if something has happened online that upsets you.

2 If you receive an upsetting message, save the message and show it to an adult.

3 Keep your personal information private. Personal information includes your name, address or school. Be careful about posting photos that might include your school uniform or school logo.

4 People you meet online can be helpful and friendly. However, you need to be careful just like when you are meeting someone new face to face. Always tell a trusted adult if someone asks to meet you.

5 Only send photos to people you trust. Always ask permission to share a photo of someone else.

6 Check your privacy settings on social media and mobile devices. Make sure you are not giving away too much information about yourself. For example, the location settings can share information about where you live or visit regularly.

7 Report anything you think may be unsafe. Visit the www.thinkuknow.co.uk website to find out more about staying safe online. On the Thinkuknow website, you can click the Report Abuse button to report issues.

 Click to report

A useful way of staying safe online is to use the SMART rules from the Kidsmart website:

www.kidsmart.org.uk/beingsmart/

Kidsmart is made by Childnet International, an organisation that wants to make the Internet a great and safe place for children (www.childnet.com).

The SMART rules cover these points.

- **Safe:** keep safe by being careful not to give out personal information when you're chatting or posting online. Personal information includes your email address, phone number and password.
- **Meeting:** meeting someone you have only been in touch with online can be dangerous. Only do so with your parents' or carers' permission. Even then, only meet someone online when your parent or carer can be present. Remember that online friends are still strangers even if you have been talking to them for a long time.
- **Accepting:** accepting emails, instant messages, or opening files, pictures or texts from people you don't know or trust can lead to problems. These may contain viruses or nasty messages!
- **Reliable:** people online might lie about who they are and information on the Internet may not be true. Always check information with other websites, books or someone who knows. If you like chatting online, it is best to only chat to your real-world friends and family.
- **Tell:** tell your parent, carer or another trusted adult if someone or something makes you feel uncomfortable or worried. Remember to tell that adult if you or someone you know is being bullied online.

⊕ Now you do it...

1 Look at the Kidsmart website for **e-safety** advice:
www.kidsmart.org.uk/beingsmart/

2 Work with a partner and read about what it means to stay SMART.

3 Create an action for each letter in SMART. For example, for 'Tell', your action could be to point to your mouth.

4 Take a photo or video of your action for each letter.

5 Put your photos or videos together to create an advert that advises students at your school how to be SMART.

If you have time...

How would you explain online safety? Would the advice you give to a 10-year-old be the same as your advice to a 20-year-old? What advice would you give a 50-year-old?

 ## Test yourself...

1 What does SMART stand for?
2 Where should you go for help if you are upset by something happening online?
3 What is the difference between a chat room and a forum?
4 Why is there more than one form of social media? Why do people have both Facebook and Twitter accounts, instead of just one?

FACT

Passwords

Passwords can protect you and your data. Longer passwords are harder to guess. Make sure your password is at least eight characters long. Mix symbols, numbers, upper-case and lower-case letters.

Key words

e-safety: E-safety means learning about the benefits and dangers of being online. Practising e-safety helps you protect yourself from online crime and anything you see online that might upset you.

Social networks: A social network is a website or other technology that lets people communicate over the Internet. People communicate informally with others who have similar interests to their own.

5.6 Watch out!

Learning outcomes

When you have completed this lesson you will be able to:

↗ stay safe online.

Learn about...

In Lesson 5.5 you learned ways to stay safe online. Have you sent an email today? Over two million emails are sent around the world every second. Sending email is a great way to share information. Images, videos and other files can be attached to emails. However, there can be some dangers when using email. The text in the email may be used to deceive another person. The attachments might contain software that tries to steal information from your computer. When using email, you need to be careful to keep safe.

You are going to learn about some of the ways people can try to trick you online. Online tricks include: phishing and spam, malware, ransomware, viruses and spyware. Someone who tries to access your device illegally is called a hacker. Once hackers have access to your account, they can steal or change your data.

Phishing and spam

You saw in Chapter 1, Computational thinking, that spam is unwanted or junk mail that is sent to a large number of people. Spam often advertises something. For example, a spam email might contain an offer for a new product.

Phishing is way to trick you into giving personal information, such as your username and password. An email might promise you a prize or money if you respond. If you reply, then the sender might ask you for your personal information. Sometimes people receive an email that looks as if it is from their bank, saying their account has been hacked. The email tells them to click a link to log into their account. All of the information and logos might look correct. However, the link is false and takes people to the hacker's website. The hacker can then record those people's usernames and passwords. If you receive an email from a bank, do not click the link in the email. Go to the bank's website and log in there. You can also phone the bank to tell the staff you have received an email and ask them to check the details.

You should never reply to these types of uninvited email. Clicking the link in the spam or phishing email might let viruses and malware onto your computer.

Malware

Malware is software designed to cause damage to your computer or your data. Once active on your computer, malware might install a virus, bother you with unwanted adverts or steal your personal information. The hacker who has stolen your data can pretend to be you and then steal your identity. When someone else uses your information to create a fake profile, this is called identity fraud. The hacker who has stolen your identity can pretend to be you to get your personal information. The hacker might even be able to get into your bank account and steal your money.

Ransomware

A recent type of malware is ransomware. When ransomware has access to your computer it encrypts your data, which means you cannot use your own data anymore. The hacker who has encrypted your data can threaten to delete your information unless you pay money, called a ransom. If you pay the ransom to the hacker attacking your computer, you may be sent a password to unlock your data.

Ransomware is one of the ways a hacker might try to steal your data

Viruses

When installed, a computer virus infects your computer, similar to the way a human virus infects your body. A virus can make your computer run slowly, damage your data and make your computer unusable. Some viruses can even steal your data. A virus will try to send itself to your contacts through email or file sharing. By sending itself to your contacts, a virus can spread quickly.

Spyware

Spyware is software that installs itself without your knowledge. Spyware can sometimes be part of other software that you install. Spyware can steal your personal data, such as your username and password. Hackers can then use the information to access your bank account. They can also sell your personal information, such as your address and phone number, to private companies.

 **How to...**

You can take steps to protect yourself and your data.

Remember to be SMART—use your common sense

You have already learned not to give out your personal information and to judge actions based on being SMART. There are also technologies that you can use to protect yourself.

Antivirus software computer

Antivirus software will stop malware from installing and becoming active on your computer. You can download free antivirus software. Many major banks provide a link to antivirus software from their website.

Antivirus software that you pay for is often more powerful than antivirus software that is free. Paid-for antivirus software has no advertising. Paid-for antivirus software has more tools than free antivirus software to stop a virus from installing on your computer.

Firewall

Some operating systems have a **firewall** included. A firewall is software that checks the connections between your computer and the Internet. The firewall will stop the connection if it identifies something suspicious. Make sure you turn the firewall on.

Password managers

Make sure you have different passwords for different sites. Having many passwords can be hard to remember. You can use a password manager, such as Lastpass or Dashlane, to help you create and store good passwords. You only need to remember one password for your password manager. The password manager will then give you the login password for each website you need.

Now you do it...

- ↗ Describe one method of protecting your computer against a virus.
- ↗ Explain how putting personal information online might put you and your money at risk.
- ↗ What is the best way to protect yourself online, and why?

If you have time...

Use a trusted website to investigate the most common types of virus.

 ## Test yourself...

1   How can you protect yourself against a person who is phishing?
2   Explain two ways in which you can protect yourself online.
3   What is the difference between malware and ransomware?
4   Why would a person create a virus?

FACT

The Creeper virus

The Creeper virus was the first virus ever detected. The Creeper virus was not designed to damage, but to show the message, 'I'm the creeper, catch me if you can!' A program called The Reaper was created to remove it.

Key words

Malware: Malware is software designed to cause damage to your computer.

Phishing: Phishing is tricking someone to give personal information which might then be used for criminal activity.

Firewall: A firewall is software designed to protect your computer by monitoring and controlling access.

Review what you have learned about information technology

Overview

In this chapter you have learned how to:

↗ explain the difference between a manual and automatic input device

↗ describe a variety of external input, output and storage devices

↗ explain and give examples of system and application software

↗ explain the relationship between user, software and hardware

↗ describe different types of computer network and explain their advantages and disadvantages

↗ describe e-safety

↗ understand where to get help if you need it

↗ stay safe online.

 Test questions

Answer these questions to check how well you learned this topic.

1 What is an input device?

2 Give an example of a manual input device and explain what it does.

3 Why might an automatic input device be better than a manual input device?

4 Name and describe three output devices.

5 Name a piece of hardware that is both an input and an output device.

6 What does an operating system do?

7 Describe three types of LAN.

8 What does SMART stand for?

9 What is phishing?

10 Where should you go for help if you are upset by something happening online?

Assessment activities

Starter activity

Think about the computers you see every day. Each one may look slightly different, but they all have input and output devices.

1. Write the name of each device labelled from 'a' to 'g' in this picture. Write whether each is an input, output or storage device.

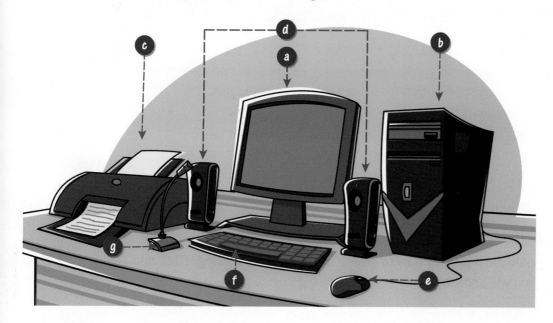

2. Draw a picture of a tablet computer. Label the input and output parts.
3. Find out which operating system your school computers use.

Intermediate activity

Every day you use networks to connect to the Internet. Your home and school may contain a network. You also may use a mobile phone to connect to the Internet.

↗ Draw a cartoon to show your normal day using technology.

↗ Your cartoon should start from when you wake up and finish when you go to sleep.

↗ Add detail to the cartoon to show which networks you are using.

Extension activity

What do the letters stand for in SMART? Write a short sentence to explain each letter.

Creative Communication

Create a website

Overview

You have learned that app is short for application software. Phones and other mobile devices run apps. An app is a set of instructions that control the computer. The instructions make the computer carry out a task.

We no longer need to write code to create simple websites, but having a basic understanding of HyperText Language Markup (HTML) helps us create or edit web pages.

In this chapter you will learn to use HTML tags to create a web page. You will also use Microsoft Expression Web 4 to create a website of two or more pages.

Learning outcomes

By the end of this chapter you will know how to create simple websites using HTML and web design software. You will know how to:

- ↗ create and edit a basic web page
- ↗ describe HTML
- ↗ identify basic HTML tags
- ↗ describe good web design
- ↗ sketch a wireframe design for your web page
- ↗ use images and hyperlinks on your web page.

Talk about...

Find a partner and discuss your favourite websites. Think about these questions.

- What attracted you to each website?
- Do your favourite websites share common features?
- What do you think makes a good website?

F|A|C|T

Who is Sir Timothy John Berners-Lee?

Tim Berners-Lee is widely known as the creator of the World Wide Web and the main author of HTML. He was born in London, England in 1955 and graduated from Oxford University in 1976. Tim Berners-Lee built his first computer at Oxford. He built the computer using parts of a TV set, among other items. While working in a physics laboratory called CERN in Geneva, Switzerland, Tim Berners-Lee created the World Wide Web. He launched the world's first website `http://info.cern.ch` on 6 August 1991.

HTML
Ordered lists
Hyperlink
Wireframe
Unordered lists
Nesting   House style   **Tag**   Content
Online   **Web browser**   Creative   Website
Graphic   Code   Design   **Navigation**
Layout
Home page   **Copyright**
Communication
Text editor

6.1 Starting HTML

Learning outcomes

In this chapter you will create your own website using Microsoft Expression Web 4 or other suitable software. Before you do that, you will need to understand some basic HTML concepts.

When you have completed this lesson you will be able to:

↗ describe HTML

↗ identify basic HTML tags used in a website's source code

↗ use HTML to create the basic structure of a web page.

⌘ Learn about...

HTML is used to create web pages. HTML uses **tags** and elements to create the basic structure of a web page. Elements are used to control how the text appears on your web page. A tag is a command that defines the beginning and the end of an element. Tags can be used to create headings, paragraphs, images, hyperlinks and much more.

A **web browser** is the software used to access a web page. Internet Explorer, Safari and Firefox are examples of web browsers. The code used to create web pages can be seen by viewing the source code of that page. The way you access the source code will depend on your web browser.

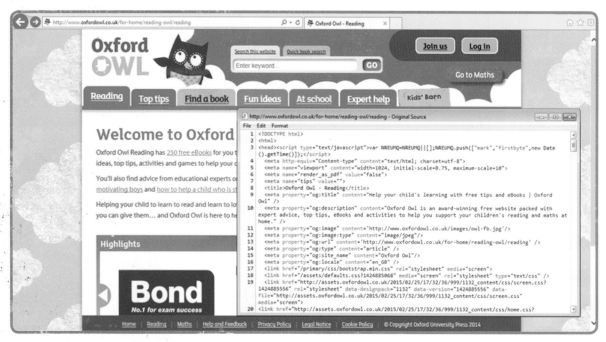

Microsoft Expression Web 4 and Adobe Dreamweaver are examples of professional HTML editors.

An HTML editor is software that lets you create and edit web pages. There are many online applications that help you write and edit HTML, but all you need is a basic text editor such as Notepad for Microsoft Windows or TextEdit for Apple Mac.

The syntax is the set of rules that HTML uses to communicate with the browser. Here are some simple rules and tags that will help you create the structure of a basic web page. A web browser reads HTML source code to display it as a web page.

Tips for working with tags

- A tag is an HTML command. Elements and their tags create the basic structure of your web page.

- Tags must always be enclosed in angle brackets < >, for example, <body> and </body>

- Most tags come in pairs. Always remember to open and then close your tags.

- Opening tags have angle brackets <html>

- Closing tags have a forward slash within the angle bracket </html>

- HTML can be written in upper-case or lower-case letters. Choose one case and stick to it.

- Spelling is important. If tags are spelled incorrectly the browser will not understand the tag.

 How to...

You need these tags to create the basic structure of a web page.

The examples in this chapter show tags in colour to make it easy for you to follow. Do not expect to see colours in your HTML editor.

Basic structure of a web page

DOCTYPE declaration < !DOCTYPE html > : tells the browser what language it is reading by defining the document type. Here, it is HTML.

It must be the first tag on your page. This tag does not need to be closed.

HTML tags < html > </html > : identify the beginning and the end of the page. The entire page will be written between these two tags.

```
< !DOCTYPE html >
< html >
< head >  < /head >
    < body >
    < /body >
< /html >
```

The basic structure of a web page

The opening tag < html > should be placed after the declaration.
The closing tag < /html > must be placed last on the web page.

Head tags < head > < /head > : give information about the document. Head tags may include browser information, set the styles and give other invisible information.

You must only use the head tag once. Use it after the opening HTML tag.

Body tags < body > < /body > : the text or images between these tags will be visible on your web page. Only use the body tags once. The body tags are indented to make editing easier.

Use body tags after the closing head tag and before the closing HTML tag.

 ## Now you do it...

1   Open your favourite web page or the page shown by your teacher.
2   View the source code in Internet Explorer or another web browser.
3   Print or save this page and then highlight the DOCTYPE declaration and any other simple tags you can find. You can complete this task with a partner or on your own.

Follow these instructions to create a basic web page structure that you will use in later activities.

4   Make a folder in your work area titled Web Design.
5   Open Microsoft Notepad or another text editor.
6   Insert simple tags to create a basic web page structure.
7   Save your work as page1.txt (this will let you return to the text version of your file for easy editing).
8   Save your work again, but this time change the document type to html. Click Save As and type page1.html as the file name.

If you have time...

1   Add your name between the body tags.
2   Save your work with a new name and open the file in your web browser. You should see your name appear on the page.
3   Experiment by adding more text to this page.

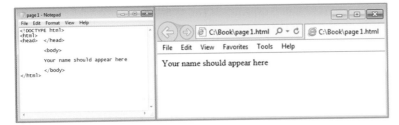

The basic structure of a web page showing text

Remember

1   Check your spelling. Your code will not work if it has spelling mistakes.

2   Make sure you have two versions of your document. One version should be .txt and the other .html

Test yourself...

1   What are HTML elements used for?
2   Name three popular web browsers.
3   Name three HTML tags and explain how these are used.
4   Define and explain syntax.

Key words

HTML: HyperText Markup Language (HTML) is used to create web pages.

Tags: A tag is a command that defines different parts of a document. Tags tell the browser how to display the information contained between the tags. Tags define the beginning and the end of an element.

Web browser: A web browser is a software application used to view or display information on the World Wide Web.

Learning outcomes

When you have completed this lesson you will be able to:

↗ use HTML to edit or create a basic web page

↗ identify basic HTML tags used in a website's source code

↗ edit your web page using a HTML editor.

⌘ Learn about...

In Lesson 6.1 you learned that HTML tags are codes used to create the basic structure of a web page. Each tag defines a different part of the document and separates the code into elements. We have already used:

↗ DOCTYPE declarations < !DOCTYPE html >

↗ HTML tags < html >

↗ head tags < head > </head >

↗ body tags < body > </body >

This lesson will examine tags in more detail and will introduce tags such as paragraph tags < p > and title tags < title >.

Tags can go inside each other, building up the detail of the web page. This is called **nesting** the tags. When you nest tags you should indent the tags to make editing easier. Remember to always close the tags in reverse order.

⏻ How to...

You can learn to add title and heading tags to your web page.

Title and heading tags

Title Tag < title > </title > : identifies what the page is called. You can see the title in the browser's title bar or tab.

The title tag should go between the **head** tags.

In this example, the title of this page is My Autobiography. The title tag within the **head** tag has also been indented. The title tag is nested.

Heading tags < h1 > </h1 > : do not confuse this with the **head**. The heading tag is similar to a paragraph heading. Using a heading tag will

```
< !DOCTYPE html >
< html >
< head >
    < title > My Autobiography  </title >
</head >
    < body >
        < h1 > Vital Statistics  </h1 >
        < h6 > My Family  </h6 >
    </body >
</html >
```

The basic structure of a web page including title and heading tags automatically make text a bold and larger font. There are six heading tags ranging from <h1> to <h6>. The heading tag <h1> will display text using the largest font for main headings while <h6> will display text in a smaller font, often used for sub-headings. In this example, the main heading is Vital Statistics.

The heading tag is placed within the body tag and it is also nested.

The sub-heading is My Family.

Paragraph tags

Once the structure of your web page is in place you can add content.

The content must be placed between the body tags and under the correct heading tags.

If you plan to include a lot of text, you will find paragraphs useful. Paragraphs give structure to your writing and help the reader to identify new ideas.

Paragraph tags <p> </p> identify the start and end of paragraphs.

The paragraph tag is placed within the body tag and below the heading tag. In this example it has also been nested to make it easier to edit.

```
<!DOCTYPE html>
<html>
<head>
   <title> My Autobiography </title>
</head>
   <body>
      <h1> Vital Statistics </h1>
      <h5> My Family </h5>
            <p> My family is made up of five people. I have two
            sisters. My rabbit is called Comet. </p>

            <p> My family live in an apartment in the city. We
            enjoy going on holiday to new places. </p>
   </body>
</html>
```

The basic structure of a web page including paragraph tags

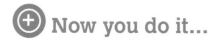

⊕ Now you do it...

1   Open page1.txt which you created in Lesson 6.1.

2   Try adding title and heading tags.

3   Try adding paragraph tags.

4   Be creative! Plan at least one paragraph about your family, friends and pets. Add further paragraphs if you have time.

5   Save your work as page1.txt

6   Save your work again, but this time change the document type to html.

7   Check your work. Navigate to your Web Design folder and open page1.html using Internet Explorer or a web browser of your choice.

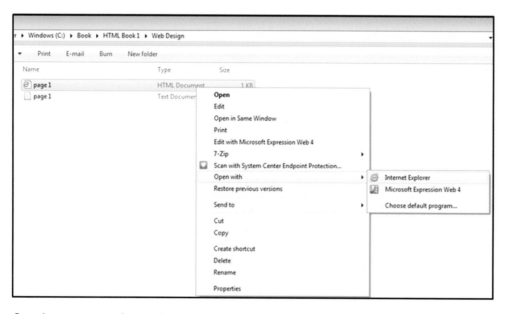

Opening your page in a web browser

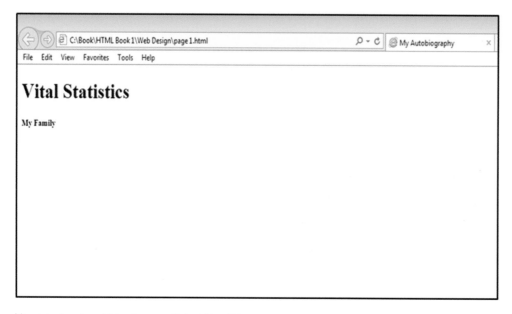

Your page should look something like this

If you have time...

You can learn more about heading tags and web browsers.

↗ Open your page1.text again and edit the heading tags to change the font size of your headings. For example, try < h4 > rather than < h5 >. What do you think looks better and why? Share your views with a partner.

↗ Can you name the popular web browsers pictured here? Use the Internet or work with a partner if you get stuck. Can you think of any browsers not listed?

Popular web browsers

Test yourself...

1 Why should you indent tags when nesting?
2 What does a paragraph tag do and how would you use it?
3 What is the difference between a head and a heading tag?
4 What is the difference between a title tag and a heading tag?

FACT

The first web browser
Sir Tim Berners-Lee created the first web browser. Sir Tim considered naming his web browser The Mine of Information and The Information Mesh. Sir Tim eventually called his web browser Nexus.

Key words

Nesting: Nesting is the way elements such as tags are put inside each other.

Formatting text

Learning outcomes

When you have completed this lesson you will be able to:

↗ use HTML to edit a basic web page

↗ identify basic HTML tags used in a website's source code

↗ describe some of the essential components of good web design

↗ edit your web page using HTML editing.

⌘ Learn about...

In Lesson 6.2 you learned about using title, heading and paragraph tags to give structure to your writing. There are many other ways to improve the look of your web page. Emphasising text adds structure to your content and helps people visiting your website to see important ideas. On average, visitors to your website take less than ten seconds to decide whether to stay on your web page. The more attractive and easy to read your web page is, the more likely it is that a visitor will take time to browse. In the future you could choose to become a web designer, or you may simply wish to design a website for yourself. Either way, you will need to understand how to make your website attractive to a large number of people. Using features such as lists, bold, italics and colour will make important parts of your web page eye-catching.

Lists

Lists are useful ways to organise information and provide structure to your web page. Lists break up text, making the words easier to scan. The most common lists are bulleted lists and numbered lists. Bulleted lists are a useful way to show information that is not ordered. Numbered lists are better to use when you are presenting information in a sequence.

⏻ How to...

You can learn how to add colour to your web page text.

The **bold tag** <b> </b> *italic tag* <i> </i> or underline tag <u> </u> should be placed on either side of the text to be formatted. These tags are opened and closed in the usual way.

Colour tags work differently because the opening and closing tags are not the same. Colour tags also use the American spelling: color. You must use the American spelling of color when writing or editing HTML or your code will contain errors. Spelling errors will result in your code being displayed incorrectly, so take care!

The opening tag <font color = blue> or <font color = red> will change depending on the colour you are using but the closing tag </font> remains the same.

> **Example:**
>
> <p> <font color = blue> Blue </font> is my favourite colour! </p>
>
> Displays as:
>
> Blue is my favourite colour!

Note that we use American spelling when writing HTML code, but we can use English spelling in the text.

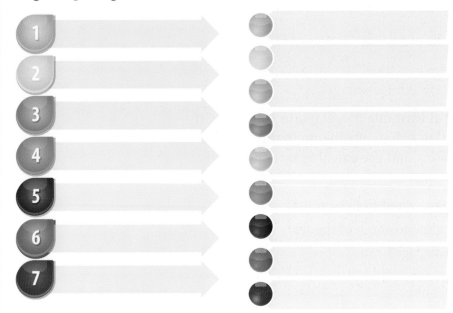

Numbered lists show information in a sequence. Bulleted lists often show information that is not in a set order.

Ordered lists < ol > will produce numbered lists. **Unordered lists** < ul > will give you bullet points. Every item you list should start with < li > and end with < /li > .

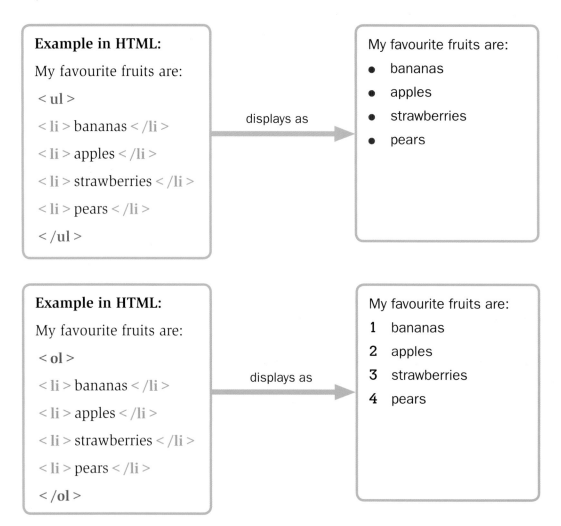

Example in HTML:

My favourite fruits are:

< ul >

< li > bananas < /li >

< li > apples < /li >

< li > strawberries < /li >

< li > pears < /li >

< /ul >

displays as

My favourite fruits are:

- bananas
- apples
- strawberries
- pears

Example in HTML:

My favourite fruits are:

< ol >

< li > bananas < /li >

< li > apples < /li >

< li > strawberries < /li >

< li > pears < /li >

< /ol >

displays as

My favourite fruits are:

1 bananas

2 apples

3 strawberries

4 pears

Top tip You can use more than one tag on any given piece of text. Remember to close the tags in reverse.

< b > < u > < i > Comet < /i > < /u > < /b >

⊕ Now you do it...

In Lesson 6.2 you should have added at least one paragraph to your page. If you have not done so, complete that task before moving on to this activity. You can make your web page more interesting and eye-catching by adding lists, colours and more.

1 Open page1.txt which you created or edited in Lesson 6.2.

2 Add tags for bold, italics and underline to some of the text.

3 Save your work as page2.txt AND as page2.html

4 View your work as a web page.

5 What information could you add as an ordered or unordered list? Perhaps you could add your favourite colours, foods, movies or music. Try this now.

6 What other information could you add to your web page? Discuss some ideas with a partner. Add two more paragraphs or lists to your page.

If you have time...

You can develop your web page further.

➤ What other information could you add to your web page? Discuss some ideas with a partner. Add two paragraphs or lists to your page.

➤ Try to nest more than one formatting tag to one piece of text.

Test yourself...

1 What is the tag used to make text bold?

2 Write out the HTML used to make the word 'happy' appear in bold and in italics.

3 Use an example to explain the difference between an ordered and unordered list.

4 Identify three errors in this code.

```
< h1 > Vital Statistics < /h1 >

      < h4 > My Family < /h5 >

< p > My family is made up of < i > five people < /i > . I have two sisters. My
< b > rabbit < /b > is called < b > < u > < i > Comet < /u > < /i > < /b > . < p/ >

< p > My family live in an < u > apartment in the city. We enjoy going on
holiday to new places.

< p >  < font color = blue > Blue < /font color > is my favourite colour! < /p >
```

FACT

World Wide Web Consortium

Today, Tim Berners-Lee is the Director of the World Wide Web Consortium. The World Wide Web Consortium is responsible for setting technical standards for the web. If you are interested in what Tim Berners-Lee has to say, you can have a look at his twitter feed: `@timberners_lee`

Key words

Ordered lists: An ordered list adds numbers to your list. You can use an ordered list to show a sequence.

Unordered lists: An unordered list is like a set of bullet points. You can use an unordered list when the sequence of the items is not important.

⌘ Learn about...

In Lesson 6.3 we explored some HTML formatting features you can use to improve the look of a website. As well as being attractive, a website should be easy to use. It should be appealing to the people who visit and use it (its audience).

Look at other websites to see what features the web designer has used to make the site attractive and easy to use. Look at the way information is presented. Think about the different layouts that web designers use. What have they done to make their website interesting to the audience?

Many web pages have standard layouts that include title, **navigation** bars, menus and an area for **content**. Navigation is the way your audience moves from page to page on your website. The content of a web page is the information on that page. Content can be text, images, video or sound.

A good website follows a house style. This means that all the pages have the same or similar layout, font types, colour schemes and language.

One of the first steps in web design is to sketch the website or create a **wireframe**. A wireframe works like a sketch. A wireframe helps you get an idea of how the website will look when it is finished. It also helps you work out how different elements of a site will work with each other.

A small project only needs a simple wireframe. You could include a place for the content, images and the menu bar. If you are planning a larger project, the wireframe could also include detail on colour, font size, font type, line spacing and hyperlinks.

⏻ How to...

You can design a wireframe for a website. If you want to look at other website wireframes, you can use a browser bookmarklet, such as Wirify. A bookmarklet is a small program that acts as a bookmark and is stored in a web browser. The Wirify bookmarklet shows the wireframe version of any active website. Looking at different websites' wireframes will show you how the sites are structured. This can help you to design your own wireframe.

The Oxford Owl website

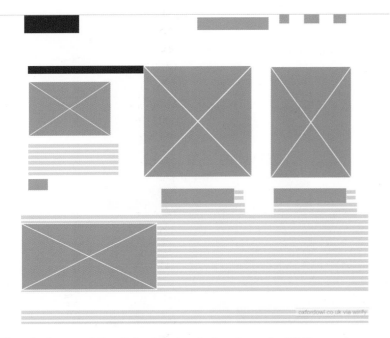

The wireframe of the Oxford Owl website shown by Wirify

When creating a wireframe you should consider these points.

↗ Purpose: is this website for business, information, advertising, personal use or education?

↗ Audience: who is the website targeting?

↗ Content: what information will appear?

↗ Appearance: what colours, fonts and styles will you use?

Tips for designing a website

1 Design the **home page** first. The home page is usually the first page of your website.

2 Keep the website simple.

3 Make the text easy to read.

4 Use only a small number of graphics because graphics may take time to load. Having to wait can be frustrating for visitors to the website.

5 Don't underline your content as visitors may think this is a broken hyperlink.

6 Keep the website easy to navigate.

⊕ Now you do it...

1   In groups or pairs, select two or three of your favourite websites for discussion.

  • What do you like about the websites and what could be improved?

  • What layout or style features appear on all the websites?

  • If you have access to a bookmarklet such as Wirify, have a look at the wireframes of the websites.

  Present your findings in a table or by using the software of your choice.

An example of a simple wireframe design

2   Think about a web page that you would like to design, or that your teacher would like you to design. Consider the purpose, audience, content and appearance. Remember to use a standard layout that includes title, navigation, menus and areas for content.

3   Write notes giving your ideas. Use your notes to sketch a wireframe. You may use a template given to you by your teacher or you may design your own.

🌐 If you have time...

↗ Create a second wireframe, considering the content you might want to include.

📄 Test yourself...

1   What four things should you consider when sketching a wireframe?
2   Why is it important to consider your audience when designing a website?
3   Give two advantages of using a wireframe.
4   What does the term 'house style' mean?

Key words

Content: Content is the information presented on a web page. Content may be text, image, video and music.

Home page: A home page is the first page of a website. This page introduces the website to an audience.

Navigation: Navigation is a visual tool that allows a user to move around a website.

Wireframe: A wireframe is a simplified diagram of a web page that shows content, navigation and images.

Learning outcomes

When you have completed this lesson you will be able to:

- ✈ use HTML to create a basic web page
- ✈ use images on your web page
- ✈ create your web page using a graphical user interface (GUI) and HTML editing.

⌘ Learn about...

Microsoft Expression Web 4 is an HTML editor that helps you design your website. Microsoft Expression Web 4 is free to download. In Microsoft Expression Web 4 you can create a web page using code such as HTML, a GUI or both. A GUI allows you to use graphics such as icons or button rather than text to interact with software. There are also many other free online tools for web design that you can try.

Microsoft
Expression Web 4

Copyright

When creating a website, you may want to use images that you have found on the Internet. These images may be subject to **copyright**. Copyright is the legal protection of someone's creative work, such as a photographer's work. You must not copy, share or use images that do not belong to you, unless you have permission from the copyright owner. If you want to download and use images from the Internet, try using a website such as:

`https://pixabay.com`

Pixabay provides images and video that you can download and use free of charge.

 **How to...**

You will learn how to design a website. All the pages and images from your site will be inside a new folder.

1 Create a local folder in your IT work area called My Website. You can usually do this by right-clicking in the File area and selecting New then Folder. The exact way you create a new folder will depend on the operating system you are using. All the pages and images from your website will be contained inside this folder.

2 Open the folder called My Website and create a subfolder called Images. This is where you will store any images you wish to use on your website.

3 Once you have done this, open Microsoft Expression Web 4.

Getting started

Follow these steps to get started. The diagram may help you.

1 Click Site, then New Site.

2 Browse to the folder you created earlier and click OK.

3 Select General, then Empty Site.

4 Right-click your folder list and create a new HTML page. Call this Home Page.

5 Double-click the Home Page to open it.

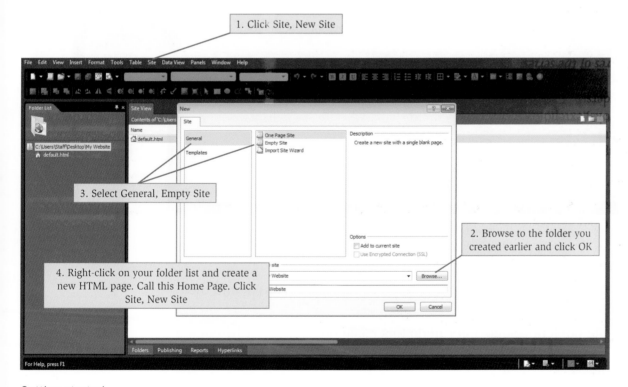

Getting started

Adding content

This website is going to be about whales and dolphins.

1 Select Split to split the screen and see the HTML.

2 Create your heading using a heading style. Remember what you learned about headings in Lesson 6.2. We have used heading 1 < h1 > for this. You can write this in HTML or use the graphic interface.

3 Write a short introduction and format this as a paragraph.

4 Create a sub-heading, again by selecting a heading style. We have used heading 3 < h3 > .

5 Create a list that will give your page structure. Microsoft Expression Web 4 will create this for you if you select bullet points, or you can use the list tag < li > .

6 Save your web page.

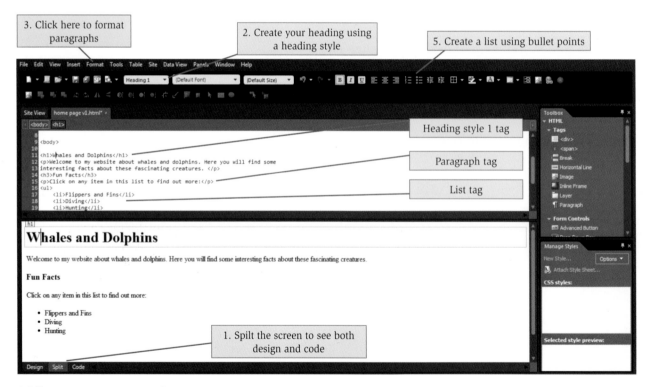

Adding content to your web page

Formatting

1 If you would like to change your background colour, select Format and then Background.

2 Try changing the font colour. You can do this using the tool bar or by editing the HTML directly.

3 Also try using bold or italics.

Inserting an image

Images can make a website interesting and fun. Inserting an image takes just a few steps.

1 Once you have found an image you would like to use, make sure you save it in the Images folder you created earlier. Then select Insert, Picture, From File and browse to the file you would like to use.

2 Right-click your image and select the Picture Toolbar. This will make it easier to edit your image.

3 Right-click your image and select picture properties. Edit your image if you wish. You will learn more about editing images in Lesson 6.6.

4 Save your page.

⊕ Now you do it...

↗ Create the first page of your own website. Select a topic of your choice, or a topic that your teacher gives you.

⊕ If you have time...

↗ Edit the HTML to change colours and list styles.

↗ Add a second image and give this a caption.

⊟ Test yourself...

1 Use an example to show how copyright rules might be broken.

2 What does GUI stand for?

3 Give an example of an HTML editor and explain what an HTML editor does.

4 Why is it important to save your images and files in a main website folder?

Key words

Copyright: Copyright is the legal protection of creative work.

Editing a web page

Learning outcomes

When you have completed this lesson you will be able to:

↗ use HTML to edit and add pages to a website

↗ use images and hyperlinks on your web page

↗ edit your web page using a GUI and HTML editing.

 **Learn about...**

Websites are made up of web pages grouped together. In Lesson 6.5 you created the structure of a website and added one page. The page you added was the home page, which introduced your website. A home page has **hyperlinks** to other pages within your website. A home page might also have hyperlinks to external websites. A hyperlink is an image, graphic or piece of text that, when you click it, links your web page to another web page.

Editing images

In order to make a website look good you may wish to edit some of the images you will be using. Microsoft Expression Web 4 lets you edit your image. If you would like a more advanced tool, you can use image editing software. There are many free tools available online. Picmonkey `www.picmonkey.com` is one example.

How to...

You can learn how to edit an image, add pages and other features to your website.

Editing an image

1 Save any images you would like to use on your website into your Image folder (which you created in Lesson 6.5).

2 Open your image in Picmonkey (or other image editing software).

3 Select the Edit button. Edit any image you want to improve.

4 Add an image and try adding text or borders. You can also add colours and rotating shapes.

5 Save this work in your Image folder.

Adding a web page

You can add another web page.

1   Open Microsoft Expression Web 4.

2   Open the page you created in Lesson 6.5.

3   Click File, New, Page. Select General, HTML.

4   Your new page will appear untitled. Click File, Save As... and navigate to your website folder. Save your page. Think of a name that fits the structure of your website. The first page from our website will be called Flippers and Fins.

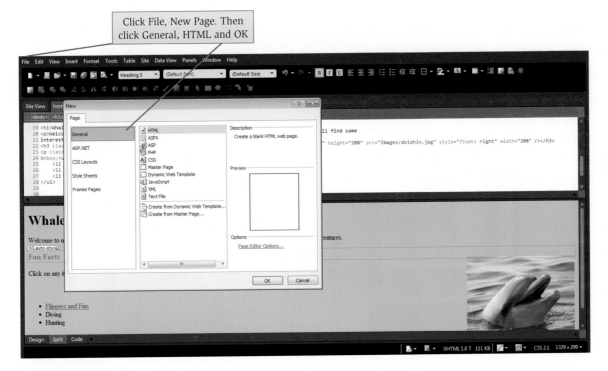

Adding a web page

Linking pages

You will see your home page. Your new page is listed in the tabs on the top of the screen.

1   Click the home page to activate it.

2   Highlight the text you want to link then right-click and select Hyperlink.

3   Browse to the appropriate file and click OK. You will notice that the text is now in blue and underlined.

4   You can test the hyperlink by following it. Select the hyperlink and hold down the Ctrl key then click your mouse. You should be taken to your new page.

5   Save your work.

You are now ready to add content to this second page.

Adding an interactive button

You can add an interactive button to take you back to your home page.

1   On your second page, click Insert, then Interactive Button.

2   Select a button of your choice and name your button.

3   Browse to your home page to link the pages.

4   Click OK.

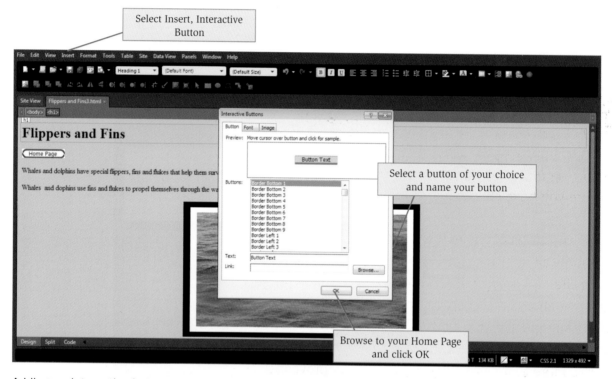

Adding an interactive button

Inserting image accessibility properties

When you insert an image you may be asked to provide accessibility properties. Accessibility properties let you add text to your image. This text is shown while your image is downloading. The text is also shown when an image can't be found and when a user hovers over the image with a mouse. This is called Alternate Text.

Adding Alternate Text will also make your image accessible to screen readers. A screen reader makes your web page accessible to visually impaired readers by reading out the text in a computerised voice. Long text describes the image in more detail.

Testing your website

Once you have completed the second page of your website you should test it.

1 Save your work and close Microsoft Expression Web 4.

2 Open your My Website folder.

3 Open your home page in Internet Explorer or another web browser.

4 Click your hyperlinks to move between different parts of your website.

⊕ Now you do it...

1 Follow the steps to create the second page of your own website.

2 Make sure you include an edited image, an interactive button and a hyperlink between your first and second page.

3 When you have finished your website, evaluate your work before moving on to the next task. Look back at your website and make sure you have checked it for errors. Ask yourself these questions.

- Have you run the spelling and grammar check?
- Have you tested your hyperlinks?
- Does the site have a logical structure?
- Did you use all of the suggested tools and features?
- Is the site suitable for its audience? How do you know?
- Does the website look good? Is it easy to use?
- If you had more time, what would you do to improve the website?

🌐 If you have time...

↗ Create more pages and try editing the HTML directly.

📃 Test yourself...

1 What is an interactive button and how is it used?

2 What is a screen reader?

3 What is the difference between a website and a web page?

4 Why is it important to add accessibility properties to an image?

Key words

Hyperlink: A hyperlink is an image, graphic or piece of text that, when clicked on, links your page to another page or document.

Review what you have learned about creative communication

Overview

In this chapter you have learned how to:

- use HTML to edit or create a web page
- describe HTML
- identify basic HTML tags used in a website's source code
- describe the essential components of good web design
- sketch a wireframe design for your web page
- use images and hyperlinks on your web page
- edit your web page using a GUI and HTML editing.

Test questions

Answer these questions to check how well you have learned this topic.

1 What is HTML and what does it stand for?

2 Identify and name the tags used in this example.

```
< !DOCTYPE html >
< html >
< body >
< h1 > My First Assessment < /h1 >
< h2 style = "color:blue;" > Identify the HTML Code < /h2 >
< p > Chapter One. < /p >
< /body >
< /html >
```

3 What is nesting?

4 Give an example of how you would nest the word 'Communication' using the tags for bold and italics.

5 Why do web designers use wireframes?

6 What is copyright?

7 Why is it useful to have a home page?

8 What should you think about when evaluating a website?

9 Here is some example text: Using headings in HTML

   How would you use HTML tags to define this text as a level 3 heading?

10 How does alternative text attached to an image help visually impaired people?

Assessment activities

You should be able to create a simple web page using HTML. You should also be able to add complex elements to your web page using the GUI.

Starter activity

1 Create a new folder called Assessment1 in your network area.
2 Open Microsoft Expression Web 4 and create a new web page called My First Assessment.
3 Type in the code shown below.
4 Change the font colour to red.
5 Save and close your page.

```
< !DOCTYPE html >
< html >
< body >
< h1 > My First Assessment < /h1 >
< h2 style = "color:blue;" > What I have learned about HTML < /h2 >
< p > Tags. < /p >
< /body >
< /html >
```

Intermediate activity

1 Open the file called My First Assessment.
2 In the section called Tags, add three key facts about tags.
3 Use three formatting features to highlight key points on your web page.
4 Use nesting on at least one piece of text.
5 Save and close your page.

Extension activity

1 Create a new page called Interesting Facts. Save this page.
2 Open the file called My First Assessment.
3 Create a button that will form a hyperlink from My First Assessment to Interesting Facts.
4 Save and close the file called My First Assessment.
5 Add any interesting facts you have learned in this chapter to your page called Interesting Facts.
6 Add a numbered list to your Interesting Facts page to show your three favourite facts.

Index